TALANOA
FOUR
PACIFIC
PLAYS

TALANOA
FOUR PACIFIC PLAYS

VELA MANUSAUTE
LOLO FONUA
LEKI JACKSON-BOURKE
`AMANAKI PRESCOTT-FALETAU
LOUISE TU`U

FOREWORD BY OLIVIA TAOUMA

LITTLE ISLAND PRESS

Copyright © little island press 2017

My Name is Pilitome copyright © 2017 Vela Manusaute
Sai ē Reunion copyright © 2017 Lolo Fonua
Inky Pinky Ponky copyright © 2017 Leki Jackson-Bourke
and `Amanaki Prescott-Faletau
Gaga: The Unmentionable copyright © 2017 Louise Tu`u

Format copyright © 2017 little island press

Published by little island press

A catalogue record for this book is available from the
National Library of New Zealand

All rights whatsoever in these plays are strictly reserved, and application
for performance, either in its entirety (including readings) or in the form
of excerpts, whether or not any admission is charged, must be made before
rehersals or publicity of any kind commences to <agency@playmarket.org.nz>.
No performance may be given unless a licence has been obtained.

Apart from any fair dealing for the purpose of private study, research,
criticism or review, as permitted under the Copyright Act, no part may be
reproduced by any process without permission.

The authors assert their moral rights in the works.

201903271435

ISBN 978 1 877484 34 6

Printed by Lightning Source

This project was made possible with support and funding
from Auckland Council.

Contents

Foreword • Olivia Taouma   vii

My Name is Pilitome • Vela Manusaute   1

Sai ē Reunion • Lolo Fonua   53

Inky Pinky Ponky • Leki Jackson-Bourke
and 'Amanaki Prescott-Faletau   103

Gaga: The Unmentionable • Louise Tu`u   177

Foreword

'*We need to write, paint, sculpt, weave, dance, sing, and think ourselves into existence. For too long other people have done it for us – and they've usually stereotyped us, or created versions of us that embody their own hang-ups and beliefs and prejudices about us. So, we have to write our own stories!*'

Albert Wendt[1]

Talanoa: Four Pacific Plays is the result of a two-year Auckland Council programme, 'Talanoa Series', developed in partnership with community publisher Little Island Press, to help writers of Pacific heritage to publish and access a wider audience. The 'Talanoa Series' consisted of five free publishing workshops for Pacific writers, held in Auckland libraries across the region in 2016. Each workshop offered free advice and guidance to participants on book design and publishing. The workshops encouraged Pacific writers working in Pacific languages to publish, and to enable readers to access to more Pacific stories.

Talanoa: Four Pacific Plays marks the completion of the 'Talanoa Series', and the successful partnership between Auckland Council and Little Island Press. The Pacific playwrights selected to be in this collection were 2016 Talanoa workshop participants at different stages of their careers. The collection celebrates and showcases four outstanding Pacific scripts and three Pacific Island languages – Sāmoan, Niuean and Tongan. All the plays interweave their languages naturally into the stories. There is a balancing act getting the mix of English and Pacific language right in these new New Zealand plays, in order to truly reflect the Pacific subjects and audience, while also endeavouring not to alienate non-speakers.

Due to the ephemeral nature of live theatre, this book creates an archive of sorts that preserves these plays, in the hope they will have a long life and wider audience.

---

1 http://creativetalanoa.com/tag/albert-wendt/, 2012.

The plays

In the early 1990s my father, the late Papalii Dr. Pita Taouma (who was an avid advocate, cultural advisor and supporter of Pacific arts), took me to watch a Pacific theatre workshop in Auckland. The name of the group was simply Pacific Theatre, under the direction of Justine Simei-Barton. There had only been one small work that was Pacific on our western stages in Auckland at that time and I had personally never seen our Pacific peoples reflected on stage or our stories told. This was a first for me and I was blown away. It was the first time I saw a young, fiery and passionate Niuean actor named Vela Manusaute perform. He was hilarious. He sharpened that great comic timing, becoming one half of the successful duo 'The Brownies', which I also got to see in their workshops and on stage through my father's involvement. Over the last few years Vela has risen to the top of his game with the international hit *The Factory*, the first Pacific musical written and directed by a Pacific person. Since then Vela has come back to his roots and Niuean language to write, direct and stage Niuean plays. His plays tell Niuean stories and speak the Niuean language in a western theatre setting in a way that is relatable and enjoyable for a diverse range of people.

Vela's work *My Name Is Pilitome* is very funny, comedy being Vela's strength. It is his first Niuean work, which pays tribute to his village, Mutalau. I first saw this work live in 2014 at the Corban Estate Arts Centre. I loved the hilarious miscommunications and lost-in-translation moments. A lot of Niuean language is spoken, but there is enough English to keep the rest of us laughing out loud. The audience had a large Niuean presence, but also a mix of other ethnicities. It was heart-warming to see people paying to see and clearly enjoying plays about Pacific Islanders that use a lot of non-English dialogue.

Louise Tu`u on the other hand approaches comedy in a very different way. She is Sāmoan and unconventional in many ways, but is just as much a staunch storyteller of Pacific stories, characters and social injustices as Vela is. She speaks Sāmoan, German, Italian and English, and was the first New Zealand or Pacific Island playwright to be awarded the Royal Court International Theatre Residency in London as a Chevening Fellow in 2005. In 2007, her play *Imakulata* became the first Sāmoan/New Zealand work presented at the World Indigenous Theatre Reading Series at the Martin E. Segal Center in New York. She is accomplished, but she is also hilarious. Louise has a great sarcastic wit and warmth that shines through in her theatre. Louise often performs her work outside the conventional western theatre space, instead preferring community spaces and halls.

Gaga: The Unmentionable is a good example of this. Performed in 2012 at the Auckland Old Folks' Association hall on Gundry Street off Auckland's Karangahape Road, I experienced the work close up. It was 'poor theatre' at its best, but once Louise Tu`u's Sāmoan mother took to the stage the play took flight. She became for me the centre, the matriarch who anchored the play in its Pacific roots. She had me laughing out loud, seeing the universal push-pull relationship between mother and daughter. The written version includes English translations of the Sāmoan dialogue, which do not exist in the live play. This makes the written play easier for non-Sāmoan speakers to follow. My favourite scene describes different uses of the ie lavalava, something we enjoyed as Pacific Island children.

Over the past decade we have had a surge in Tongan theatre, written, acted and directed by Tongans, with Suli Moa, Sesilia Pusiaki and Lolo Fonua at the forefront. Lolo's *Sai ē Reunion* has been very successful. She interweaves the Tongan language with English resulting in a realistic portrait of Tongan characters living in New Zealand. 'Sai ē' means 'Good, eh' in English, and is used in a sarcastic context. Lolo writes beautifully for a Tongan audience, but also presents many family and social issues as universal experiences. I have seen this play performed live at the Ōtara Music Arts Centre with a primarily Tongan audience. I laughed the whole way through, as did the rest of the crowd. Even though I don't speak Tongan, I could still follow the story. I love how the play brings two Tongan worlds together – a girl fresh from Tonga who doesn't speak much English and two New Zealand Tongans who don't speak much of their native language. It offers the audience an inside view of family life for young Tongan girls living in New Zealand. Lolo Fonua is a much-needed voice in our Pacific theatre community.

The Pacific theatre community in Auckland is small. We all know each other and many of us, including myself, have been around since its inception in the early 1990s. It is a growing community as we now have many graduates emerging from the growing number of institutes offering drama/theatre studies. It is also a fickle industry with ebbs and flows, highs and lows that have seen many companies, groups and individuals come and go. It has also meant that a few Pacific actors have performed in many of our Pacific plays over the years.

Therefore, it is not unusual that one name repeatedly arises in relation to each of the plays. That name is Leki Jackson-Bourke. He is a talented actor who has performed in many Pacific and non-Pacific plays since his graduation from the Pacific Institute of Performing Arts in 2012. Leki is also an emerging playwright. His first play *Inky Pinky Ponky* was co-written with ʻAmanaki Prescott-Faletau and developed through Lima Productions, a Creative New Zealand-funded Pacific writing workshop, in 2014. It was then picked up and developed by the Auckland Theatre Company who staged the play as part of their annual 'Next Big Thing' series in 2015. It was a success and gave people insight into the experience of Pacific pupils in New Zealand high schools, as well as providing a transgender perspective.

Talanoa – Four Pacific Plays offers a depiction of new and established Pacific voices, and worlds within Auckland and New Zealand. The collection is a reflection of how diverse our Pacific people are and also how similar, with comedy the connecting thread that runs through everything. Our Pacific languages are showcased throughout the book, reflecting our Pacific peoples through characters and experiences – writing ourselves into existence.

I must acknowledge and thank Little Island Press for all their great work throughout the 'Talanoa Series' and the development of this publication.

I also want to acknowledge Auckland Council for supporting the original workshop series, and for their commitment to the creation of this book.

Manuia le faitauga,

Olivia Taouma
Pasifika artist and producer

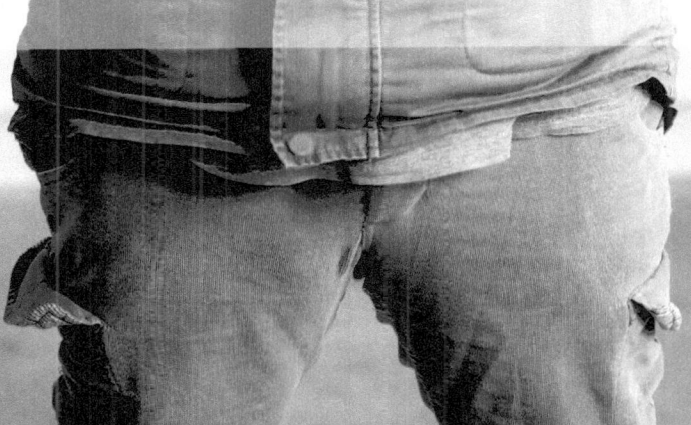

MY NAME IS PILITOME

VELA MANUSAUTE

My Name is Pilitome

Written by Vela Manusaute

About the author

Vela Manusaute is a writer and director born on Niue Island who moved to New Zealand in 1979. His passion for drama began at high school and he joined Pacific Theatre in 1987, which toured the country performing to schools. He graduated from Toi Whakaari New Zealand Drama School in 1996. His first play was *The Taro King* (2002), which led to the formation of the Kila Kokonut Krew entertainment company. Kila Kokonut Krew has produced a number of successful works, including, *Players' Night*, *Once Were Samoans* and the first Pacific stage musical, *The Factory*, which toured Australia and Edinburgh in 2014. Vela was also the executive producer for a web series of *The Factory*. He was a joint recipient of a New Generation Award for Kila Kokonut Krew, alongside his partner Anapela Polataivao, at the Westpac New Zealand Arts Awards, 2014. *My Name is Pilitome* is his first Niuean work. In 2017, Vela directed his first short film *The Messiah*, commissioned by New Zealand Film Commission, inspired by his own experience growing up.

Synopsis

Filimoana Peniamina's parents left Niue for New Zealand in 1976 and never returned home. Thirty-eight years later, their son Filimoana reluctantly returns to his parent's homeland for a hilarious journey of discovery – where he reconnects with the land, his family and makes peace with his ancestor.

Dedication

For my three kids, Rocky, Iuni and Halamoana Manusaute.

Acknowledgements

Thanks to: Kila Kokonut Krew, *From the Pacific We Rise* – Anapela Polataivao, Stacey Leilua, Aleni Tufuga and Glen Jackson; Elaine Jackson; Families, friends and all our supporters; The original cast: Joshua Iosefo, Haanz Faavae Jackson, Leki Jackson-Bourke, Tim Mitipelo and Aisea Latu; Io Aleke Faavae; The Village of Mutalau; Frank Sioneholo, Niue Arts Festival; Dr Colin Tukuitonga; Malama Makatogia Nilau, MUMT; Niue Ogo Motu, Fakatumau e Mafola – *Matakau Tufuga Fakamotu* (1976). Olivia Taouma.

First performance

My Name is Pilitome had three successful seasons in Auckland before being invited to perform at the Niue Arts and Culture Festival in 2015.

Cast

FILIMOANA: Joshua Iosefo
AUNTY LETA: Glen Jackson
TAU: Leki Jackson-Bourke
TONGA/CHORUS: Aisea Latu
KALA: Tim Mitipelo
CHORUS/MINISTER/ELDER/ELAVISI/GRANDFATHER:
    Haanz Fa`avae-Jackson

Crew

NIUE TRANSLATIONS AND CULTURAL ADVISOR: Io Aleke Fa`avae
SONGS/MUSIC: Glen Jackson
SCRIPT EDITOR/DRAMATURG: Anapela Polataivao

My Name is Pilitome

Scene 1

Niue Island. The stage is dark. Beautiful singing voices can be heard from offstage as the lights slowly come up to give the stage a golden tropical sunshine feel.

VOICES: O, O, O mai. E tau atu motu. He atu Pasifika. Kia, kia lologo fiafia, fiafia. Kia, kia lologo fiafia, fiafia. Fakatumau fakafeofanaki fakalataha.

AUNTY LETA (played by a man) enters, a drama queen in a red hibiscus dress that goes with her afro wig. She looks stunning as she leads the song, smiling and waving to the welcoming audience.

She is followed closely by two youths (CHORUS) wearing colourful lavalava with white singlet tops. The two youths shadow Aunty Leta's every move and echo some of her dialogue

Aunty's parade is interrupted by FILIMO ANA, aka Fili G, wearing jeans and a black t-shirt with a black bandana over his head. A typical wannabe gangster from South Auckland. He's just arrived from New Zealand. It's hot and he's trying to find somewhere cool to stand.

Aunty Leta and the two chorus members watch Fili G pace up and down the stage. Aunty points to Fili G. She calls out.

AUNTY LETA: Ko hai a koe?

Fili notices Aunty Leta.

FILI: I'm sorry. You talking to me?

Aunty Leta smiles.

AUNTY LETA: Who are you?

FILI: I don't talk to strangers.

CHORUS: Fia lauka ma, Aunty.

The Chorus makes a move to give Fili G a hiding. Aunty Leta pulls them back.

AUNTY LETA: Leave him.

FILI: It hot here. I'm burning. Get me some water, beer or something, old lady. Do you guys speak English here? I really need some water. This heat is killing me. I need something to drink. [To the chorus]: What you bloody shits looking at?

CHORUS: Bloody shits! He just called you 'bloody shit', ma aunty. Can we give him some bloody shit around his ears?

Aunty Leta just smiles and rubs her hands together.

AUNTY LETA: Not, now. Your mum is from Muta—

Fili G rudely cuts her off.

FILI: Mudda what? Who's your mudda?

AUNTY: Mutalau. Our village.

CHORUS (sing): Ululauta, ne hake mai e maama ki luga.

AUNTY: Mutalau, Ululauta. Where the gospel came to Niue. You know?

CHORUS: God bless, young man!

FILI: I don't go to church.

CHORUS: You will go to church. You will read your Bible while you here.

FILI: What?

CHORUS: You want a 'what' on your mouth?

The chorus move towards Filimoana.

FILI: Try me!

Fili strikes a karate pose.

AUNTY: Your father is from the village of Hakupu. He met your mother, got married and lived in Mutalau.

FILI: So?

Aunty Leta laughs.

AUNTY: So, you are Fili. I heard that you're ulu uka, Kafilo!

FILI: Ulu? I don't care.

Filimoana tries to get away from Aunty Leta and the chorus. He walks offstage. Aunty Leta calls out to the young boy.

AUNTY: Filimoana Peniamina!

Filimoana comes running back in a hurry.

FILI: My name is Fili G, old lady!

AUNTY: Your full name is Filimoana Pineneloa Sagapine Hakemai e Maama Maka Fitu.

FILI: OMG! Please don't tell me I have one of those freshie names!

AUNTY: You were named after the great missionary Peniamina who brought the gospel to the island of Niue.

FILI: I come from Mangere 275, my hood, my Nika. I'm waiting for some Niuean people to pick me up. Where are they? [Pointing to the two chorus members.] Who you guys anyway?

CHORUS ONE: I'm her mind.

CHORUS TWO: I'm her shadow.

AUNTY: And I'm Aunty Leta!

Aunty Leta does a little comedy dance.

FILI: And I'm losing my mind. I need to leave this place right now.

Aunty Leta and Chorus laugh.

CHORUS/AUNTY: 'I need to leave this place, right now.'

CHORUS ONE (to audience): He wants to leave the island!

CHORUS TWO (to audience): Like, right now.

AUNTY (to audience): No one leaves the island. We love it here!

CHORUS: Go on and swim back to New Zealand! [Laugh heartily.]

FILI: Who are you guys really?

CHORUS (in Australian accents): We told you, mate. I'm her mind. And I'm her shadow. And this is Aunty Leta! We here to pick you up!

AUNTY: Fakaaue lahi mahaki!

Fili G assesses Aunty Leta – in particular, her beard.

FILI: So . . . you my uncle?

AUNTY: Your aunty, ma bloody sid!

FILI: Aunty Leta? I don't remember my mum telling me about you. I've never seen you in any of the family photos back at home.

AUNTY: Really [straightening her wig]? No photos of me on the living room walls? But why? Because they have always been jealous of your beautiful aunty, ma son!

FILI: I'm not your son!

CHORUS: Fili G, mimi kogo! [Raise their hands to give Fili G a backhand.]

FILI: Hey, look, I have a phone with a camera. Let's take a photo for the family back home. You guys like that? What a wonderful experience I'm having with the natives.

CHORUS: We are not natives, mate. We are Niueans.

FILI: Right. Cool. Photo time.

AUNTY: Good boy. Haia homo a ia.

Fili G gives his phone to one of the Chorus to take the photo. He pose with Aunty Leta.

AUNTY: One . . . two . . . three!

CHORUS: Haia!

Fili G waits for his phone to be returned.

AUNTY: Please give his camera back.

The Chorus gives his phone back. Aunty Leta rubs her hands together in anticipation.

AUNTY: Did your mother give you anything for me?

FILI: Oh right, I see.

Fili G takes out an envelope from his pocket. You can smell the greed in the air as the Chorus points to the envelope. Aunty Leta's eye widen with excitement.

CHORUS: Haia!

AUNTY: Beautiful!

FILI: She said to give it to the right person.

CHORUS ONE: That will be me.

CHORUS TWO: That's me. Thank you, young man.

Aunty Leta gets to the envelope first. She takes it from Filimoana.

AUNTY: Thank you, my nephew.

She quickly opens the envelope and finds $100. She shakes the envelope close to her ear. She slides up to Filimoana, holding the envelope.

AUNTY: Is this all?

FILI: Yeah, I think so. Why? Is everything alright?

AUNTY: No! Is your family alright in New Zealand?

FILI: What you mean?

AUNTY: Your mother send you here with just $100? You didn't open the envelope?

CHORUS (whispering to the audience): Tama kaiha!

FILI: Look, they just dropped me at the airport and said, 'Have a happy holiday son.' So, can I please have a happy holiday? Where's the clubs at? What you guys drink here? Where the chicks at, mate? What music do you guys listen to?

Aunty's clearly not happy.

AUNTY: Have you heard of the nams?

FILI: Never heard of them. What type of music they play?

AUNTY: The buzzing sounds that goes around your ears at night. That's the only music we listen to here.

CHORUS: Mosquitos! That's the only music here.

AUNTY: How many bags you bring with you?

FILI: You asks too many questions. Not even Customs asks that many questions.

AUNTY: Niue is a small place. Same people working in the airport is related to the same people working in the police station. Here we know everything. Everybody knows everything. [Aunty Leta smiles.] What's in your bag?

FILI: Just my clothes and a few books.

AUNTY: A few books? What kind of books?

FILI (under his breath): Poetry books.

AUNTY: Fefe? Pa he tree?

CHORUS: Nakai – Pa he niu! [They laugh.]

AUNTY: We thought you were in gang?

FILI: Yeah, I'm one of those brainy G's.

CHORUS (to audience): Ko e G, pikopiko!

AUNTY: Koe tama pikopiko ne hau he motu ko Aotearoa. You know your books?

CHORUS: Throw it in the bush!

AUNTY: You know your shoes?

CHORUS: Liti ke he vao!

AUNTY: You know your attitude . . .

CHORUS: Liti ki tahi!

AUNTY/CHORUS: Cause you, heart and soul, need to reconnect with the land, Fili G.

Fili G pulls out a fake gun from his bag and aims at Aunty Leta and the Chorus. They put their hands up like being held at a robbery.

FILI (under his breath): Yes and Fili G doesn't want to be here, chilling with you funny-looking people. Fili G wants to leave this Island, like right now.

CHORUS: Ae ma Filimoana.

FILI: It's Fili G!

CHORUS: Haia ma, Fili G!

AUNTY: Welcome back, Fili G.

FILI: Welcome back? But it's my first time here.

AUNTY: Your parents left and now you coming back – so, it's a welcome back.

Aunty Leta and the Chorus break into a cheesy song: Sung like a musical/ opera, but in perfect harmony.

AUNTY/CHORUS: Welcome back, welcome back, welcome back. Ae kua hemu e fuata nei, kua lata ke keli.

FILI: Fili G!

AUNTY/CHORUS: Haia ma, Fili G! You not my girl. Oi fakalofa ma mea, fai tupe nakai ma tama? Ko fe e tau fua apala? Kua fiu au he kai timala. Welcome back, welcome back!

Fili G joins Aunty Leta and the Chorus and they all exit happily offstage.

Scene 2

The lights are low as three youths enter the stage. The leader of the three is TAU (19) who carries a rifle, followed by his cousin KALA (17) with his best mate TONGA (18) who just arrived in the country a few months ago. The trio has been hunting bats all night with no luck. Finally, they spot a few bats up a tree. Like Ninja they set up the rifle. Tau takes aim at a bat and shoots. He misses.

TAU: Damn it! I missed it!

KALA: Tau, you missed 'cos we on sacred ground.

Kala is afraid. Tau jokingly aims the rifle at Kala.

TAU: Shut up, ma fuatigi.

TONGA: Sacred ground? That's no good.

TAU: Hoha ma Tonga! Don't be afraid. Let's charge forward into the forest. I'm sure more bats are up ahead. [Tau makes a move but Kala and Tonga remain still.] Aunty wants bats for dinner and we gonna get those flying fox.

KALA: Aunty know it's not bat season. Can we get a chicken or a rat?

TAU: Our aunty, who is the Queen of the village, wants a bat for dinner, so we get Aunty a bat, ma Kala. Unless you want Aunty to bat you in the face, ma bro?

KALA: But it's too early to shoot pekas.

TAU: Too early? Who told you that?

KALA: The elders in the village. You know the rules. No shooting bats for the next six months.

TONGA: There we go – no shooting bats for months. Let's turn back and go home.

TAU: Ko e matakutaku he ha? And since when did we obey our elders? Did the elders spoke with the leader of the pekas? What about the pekas? Did you hear them say 'It's too early to shoot us?' This is not 'Save the Bat' international wildlife channel. This is Niue! We shoot bats everyday! Don't make me shoot you too for talking to the bats.

KALA: Ah, no. No one talks to the bats. That sound stupid!

TONGA (to audience): I've only been on this island for about six months, but that's the most stupid thing I've ever heard on the whole of Niue. I mean, who talks to bats?

Tau catches Tonga talking to the audience. Aims the rifle at Tonga.

TAU: You calling me stupid? Nua! You calling me goagoa?

KALA: Leave him alone. He's our next-door neighbour!

TAU: You calling me stupid too? Don't take side with Tonga. [Walks towards Tonga with the rifle.] Go on, fly like a peka back to Tonga! Flap your wings back to Tonga. Ko e ha ma Tonga?

TONGA (in his Tongan accent): We all family here, Siana.

TAU: Don't speak that horse language to me. Kai Kuli!

TONGA: I thought my name was Kai Nua?

TAU: Kai nua and Kai kuli – they're both animals with four legs, Tonga!

Tonga laughs but Tau clearly doesn't see the funny side.

TAU: Really? You making fun of it now?

TONGA: Yep, plenty of stupid, I mean crazy . . . stupid people in Tonga. Siana, maybe you're Tongan?

KALA: I told him that! I told him that . . . maybe . . .

TAU: Shut up! I'm not Tongan.

KALA: Or maybe you're Puaka from Liku!

Tonga and Kala acts like pigs, making pigs sounds. Tau points the gun to the both of them.

TAU: That's my dad's village.

KALA: Sorry, ma bro.

Pause. Tau looks at Tonga. Tau summons Kala over to his side. Points to Tonga.

TAU: He's just another Tongan looking for his passport to New Zealand by using Niue. Right, kai nua?

Tau and Kala freeze as Tonga talks to the audience.

TONGA (to audience): He's right! I really want to go to New Zealand, but I got no passport. My only way out of Tonga is to go through this stupid little Island.

Tau breaks from the freeze.

TAU: What did you say?

Tau pulls the rifle trigger back with the gun aiming towards Tonga balls.

TONGA: I Love Niue! I love all Niuean beautiful people.

A voice is heard offstage. They all recognise the voice, it is the keeper of the forest. The youths try to find a place to hide.

Enter an ELDER, the same actor who plays Chorus One from the start. The elder looks around the stage. He wears a straw hat and looks like a scarecrow. He sees the three youths pretending to be trees. The elder kicks one of the boys in the backside.

ELDER: What you people doing in my forest?

TAU: Fakaalofa lahi atu kia koe ma olu.

ELDER: What's your name?

TAU: Ko e higoa haaku ko, Tau.

ELDER: Tau he Maka?

TAU: Tau he Maka.

The old man disarms Tau with lightning speed. He then aims the gun at Tau. The boys are in awe.

ELDER: The next time you mimi on my trees.

TAU: What you want me to do? Hold it till I get home?

ELDER: Don't piss on the sacred ground or else I'm gonna chop your balls off!

The boys laugh.

ELDER: Ko e kata he ha? That goes for you all. Piss on this ground and your balls will fall. And don't touch my children! The flying fox are sacred animals of the forest, not for your bellies. Huvalu is crying 'cos your real animals are killing her children. Leave the bats alone. Go and eat a chicken – plenty of wild chicken outside the forest. Understand?

The old man hands Tau back his rifle.

Tau: Understood, Sir.

Elder: Now, get out of my forest.

The boys leave in a hurry. The elder watches the boys exit the stage. He looks up to the tree full of bats. He points his finger to the tree and shoots. A bat falls from the tree. He smiles at the audience. He picks the flying fox up and carries it offstage, laughing.

Scene 3

The village of Mutalau. Lots of empty houses. Aunty Leta walks onstage carrying a table. She places the table at centre stage. Filimoana follows behind her, recoding on his phone what he sees on the way.

FILI: So many empty houses. Where did everyone go?

AUNTY: Everyone on holiday in New Zealand. We still waiting on them to come back home to attend to their houses. I mean, look at the state of some of them. They need to be destroyed. 'Leave our houses alone, we coming back.' That's why it's good to see young people like you coming back home to fill these houses with life.

FILI: I'm not living here. I'm just here for a holiday. Do you guys have hot water? I only shower with hot water.

AUNTY: We got plenty of hot water.

FILI: What about the toilets? My father says you have to dig a hole, right?

AUNTY: We got palagi toilets now with remote control.

FILI: Remote control? Gummon! Good. You got palagi toilet papers too?

AUNTY: Palagi newspapers!

FILI: Newspaper?

AUNTY: Sandpapers! Just jokes. [For a moment they laugh, sharing dry jokes.] Come, you see that house? That's your family house.

FILI: Honest to who? That's my family house? I thought we were rich.

AUNTY: Your family is rich with weeds and cobwebs, Filimoana.

FILI: Call me Fili G.

AUNTY: Fili G, your parents left this place with The Matakau Tufuga Fakamotu in 1976. The cultural group that went to Rotorua. [Sings:] 'Kua tolotolo mai, kua tolotolo mai ke fonua fuluola nei, Rotorua, Rotorua Aotearoa!'

FILI: That's my father's song. When he's drunk he sings that song. I don't know the words but I remember the tune.

AUNTY: The group from this little Island won the hearts of all New Zealanders. A proud day that was for Niue. You know they never seen so many savage. Our dances and beautiful singing capture them on that day. That day belongs to Niue.

FILI: Were you in Rotorua?

AUNTY: Yes, I was there. After the festival we travel around New Zealand. It was cold. We couldn't wait to come back home. We came back but your parents never came back. We never heard from them. Only your mother came back a few years ago. She stayed in town. She only came to our village for a few hours and then left.

FILI: They had me. They said there was nothing here to come back to.

Aunty Leta sits down. She looks at Fili G.

AUNTY: How is your father?

FILI: We don't talk. We got nothing to talk about. But he's old. If he gets too old then I'll ship him to old people home.

AUNTY: Old people home – that's not our ways. Your father was one of the strongest young men back in his day.

FILI: He's very old now, my Nika.

AUNTY: My Nika?

FILI: That's my gang back at home. M.N in the house!

AUNTY: OK, my Nika. Your father need to come back home. Here we have no pressure. No stress. Life is free on the Island. Tell him to come back to his homeland. [Aunty stands up, she looks out to the audience and calls out, like she's reaching out to the Niuean people living in New Zealand to return home.] We need everyone to return back to Niue. Come back to the land of your ancestors. A warrior-like scream is heard from offstage. It's the boys returning from the hunt.

Tau, Kala and Tonga enter, chanting an old Niuean challenge.

TAU/KALA/TONGA: 'Haaku akau ulu fua miti, Ta lipilipi e ulu he toa.'

AUNTY: And look who's home, your family. Boys, meet your cousin from New Zealand, Fili.

TAU/KALA/TONGA: Pili!

AUNTY: Ko, Fili!

Kala starts to walk over to Fili but Tau stops him.

KALA: Hello, cousin.

FILI: 'Sup.

TAU: Ko e tuga e Mauli!

FILI: What you say, bro? Say it in English.

TAU: Oh, it's like that now?

FILI: Just saying. I don't speak your fresh lingo, G!

AUNTY: No fighting, boys.

Kala goes over and introduces himself.

KALA: Just call me Kala or Himu, nothing in between.

FILI: 'Sup bro. Call me Fili G.

KALA: Fili G – that's so cool, man. Now I wanna be Himu G.

TAU: Liu mai ki tua ma, Himu G!

AUNTY: And that is your other cousin Tau.

TAU: Ko e tuga e kay!

They all laugh, pointing at Fili G.

FILI: What did I say about your fresh lingo?

AUNTY: He called you gay. It's a joke on the island. No need to get angry. Everyone in Niue is always in a good old gay mood. As the saying goes here, 'Haia ma tau keis!'

TONGA: Haia ma magafaoa!

AUNTY: Ai fai magafaoa a koe ma, Nua!

Aunty chases Tonga offstage.

TONGA: Koe kia ma Fili.

Tonga exits. Tau clearly still has a problem with Fili.

TAU: So, what your business here, ma bro?

Aunty Leta comes back onstage.

AUNTY: Are you a policeman, ma Tau? What his business is none of your business. Your cousin, my nephew. Tau, just say hello to him and get to the umu. Where is the bat?

Aunty Leta pushes Tau and Kala offstage.

TAU: We only got one bat.

AUNTY: Useless! Get yourself to the umu!

Tau and Kala exit in a hurry. Aunty Leta comes back smiling.

FILI: Is he family?

AUNTY: Tau is your cousin. He's a throwback.

FILI: Throwback?

AUNTY: You know, we send them to school in New Zealand but they end up in trouble so New Zealand Police throws them back here.

Fili laughs.

FILI: Tau the throwback guy.

AUNTY: And Kala too. Throwbacks.

FILI: I'm not a throwback. I'm here on holiday.

AUNTY: Ah, don't worry about them. I can't wait for you to taste the peka. Have you ever had bat for dinner?

FILI: Bat?

AUNTY: Bat. Flying fox. Very, very delicious.

FILI: I can't eat Batman, man! Any other food on the Island?

AUNTY: You can have anything here – corned beef, steak, chocolate cake – but you already have all those back in New Zealand. So today on the menu? We have cheese peka, curry peka and my favourite, namu peka! Nananananananana Batman!

Aunty Leta dances like a bat around the stage. A loud voice is heard from offstage. It's the church minister of the village. He's preaching a verse from the Bible. Aunty Leta, in a panic, runs to get a chair just in time for the MINISTER to enter. It's the same actor who played the elder but this time as the church minister Reverend Tomaiitoafanaumaiihalatahi.

AUNTY: Fakaalofa lahi atu ma Akoako!

MINISTER: Ehk! . . . Ua moumou e magaaho haaku.

AUNTY: Fakamolmole, fai fekau ka kua ahiahi mai a koe he aho nei?

MINISTER: Ko e logona e tala ko e fai tama kelea, tama vale fia nofo he maaga haaku?

AUNTY: Fakamolemole, nakai fai tama kelea, tama vale ne fia nofo he maaga ha taua.

MINISTER: Taua?

AUNTY: Haau.

Minister looks over and sees Filimoana. The minister directs his dialogue towards Fili who just stares back blankly.

MINISTER: E . . . Satani! Tagata ne fakakite e fua apala ke he fifine telefua!

FILI: Huh? Sorry, I don't understand.

AUNTY: What the Minister Reverend Bishop Tomaitoafafanaumaihalatahi was saying was . . .

The minister cuts her off.

MINISTER: What I was saying was: Satan picked the apple from the tree of knowledge and the apple burst out loud with a question, and it said, what hast thou brought for me?

FILI: Oh nah, I only brought something for Aunty.

MINISTER: Ae! E . . . koe anty a koe ka?

AUNTY: Anty aho nei, uncle a pogi, kuli po Falaile, uga he po Faiumu!

MINISTER: Kata ti papa e tau ki.

AUNTY: Chehoo.

MINISTER: Fai lau kula nakai ne tamai he fuata? Ke lata mo e Akoako he maaga! Ke lagomataiaki aki e talaga he fale tuga ha taua, To fakatu taha setalite I luga . . . Ke kitekite e tau kifaga ke fakafiafia e tau loto he pouli he po.

AUNTY: Hako tika a koe ma akoako, Ke talaga e fale tuga he Atua, nakai ha taua . . . Ko e tala ke he lau kula? Fakamolemole, ko e lata ni mae magafaoa tote haaku.

MINISTER: Magafaoa? Magafaoa Ko e taha ni e magafaoa ne kautu he maaga nei, ha hai?

AUNTY: Haau.

MINISTER: E! Ti ko e fiha?

AUNTY: Ko e lahi ni ke fakatau taha po ke ua e fao, Tuga e tau fao ne paopao ke he tua a Iesu!

MINISTER: Ae! Tiaki e tau tala fakavai! Ko e mahani tafalalo a ia!

AUNTY: Fakamolemole, nakai fakavai au kia koe . . . Ae, kofe haaku kato ne toka he na e?

Aunty Leta pretends to look for the money

FILI: Aunty, the hundred dollars is covering your sideburns.

AUNTY: Fakaaue ma mea ke he haau a lagomatai! Ko e lima hogofulu ni ke lata mae aho.

MINISTER: Ka ko fe e taha lima hogofulu?

AUNTY: Fakaaoga tei ke fakatau e huhu, suka mo e mailo ke kai e fanau!

MINISTER: Kai e fanau? Kua lalahi tei a lautolu?! Toka ke hoge! Ae! Tau uka pihia e tau koloa ia?

AUNTY: Tau uka ni ka ha ne fakatau he fale koloa ha Siuani i Alofi!

Minister tries to snatch the money. Aunty Leta pulls the money away from the minister.

AUNTY: Fakamolemole, fai liogi nakai ke fakamonuina mai e fanau haaku?

MINISTER: E, To liogi fai he magaaho, neike he matua ha ha he lagi . . . Ke hafagi mai e tau puhio. Ke maligi mai e tau monuina loga kia koe moe e haau a magafaoa. Haia, Kuenaia. Amene.

The minister gets up quickly and walks towards Fili. Aunty Leta follows the minister.

MINISTER: And where you going? This is for the work of God. Please stay outside.

Aunty nods and goes back to her place.

MINISTER: So you are a crip? A blood? Kua pilitome nakai a koe?

Aunty runs over to help Fili.

AUNTY: Ko e mamafa he ha e tau kupu ma akoako.

MINISTER: Mamafa ni he mamafa e tau gata he vaha ia.

The minister is tired of all the preaching. Aunty is trying to be nice to the minister.

AUNTY: The food is nearly ready. Tau kua mau nakai e kai ha tatolu?

Tau, Kala and Tonga bring the cooked food wrapped in tin foil to the table. The minister smiles at the food.

AUNTY: Our good minister of the church, can you please bless the food?

Everyone gets ready for the prayer. Filimoana has no idea what's going on. Aunty slaps Fili on the neck. Fili falls off his chair.

FILI: What's that for?

AUNTY: Mosquito.

The minister begins the prayer.

MINISTER: Let's start our prayer. In the name of the father . . .

The light quickly changes to red. Only the minister is praying in silence. Aunty and the boys are fighting over the cooked bat in Kung Fu style.

TAU: Aunty, that's our peka.

AUNTY: I told you, the peka is for our guest from New Zealand.

The light flicks back to normal. We are back in the real world with the minister praying.

MINISTER: And we ask you, Lord . . .

The light flicks back to red. Tonga rushes to the table and puts his hand on the food. Aunty Leta grabs his hand a struggle of power.

TONGA: I want the takihi, Aunty.

AUNTY: That's for the minister. Tonga, why you still here?

FILI: Aunty, I really don't want the bat.

AUNTY (to Fili): The bat is for you. You must taste the bat.

KALA: Thank you, ma aunty.

Kala tries to take the bat from the table but Aunty beats him to it. While Aunty is fighting with Kala, Tonga and Tau go for the bat. Aunty takes them on at the same time.

FILI: Can we just stop it? I really don't want the bat!

AUNTY: Come on, son, it's for you. So when you go back to New Zealand, you can tell everyone you had bat for dinner.

Tonga makes one final attempt to go for the bat. He gets the bat and passes it to Kala. Angry, Aunty pulls out a fake sword and kills Kala. He dies dramatically. In shock, Tonga reacts.

TONGA: Not my Kala!

Enraged, Tonga draws his sword and charges towards Aunty Leta. She quickly cuts him in half with the sword. Tonga falls and dies dramatically.

AUNTY: When you kids gonna learn? I'm the master here!

Tau draws his weapon out and screams in rage.

TAU: I want that peka, old lady!

AUNTY: Then come for it, grasshopper!

Tau draws his sword and charges towards Aunty Leta. Aunty Leta strikes but misses Tau.

TAU: You getting old, master!

Tau laughs. Aunty Leta laughs louder. Tau realises that he's been hit. His body crumples. In agony he dies a dramatic death. All three boys are lying on the ground, dead. Aunty Leta takes the bat and places it back on the table.

AUNTY: I told you, this bat is for Fili.

The lights flick back to normal. The boys quickly get up and return back to their places.

MINISTER: In the name of the father. Amene.

EVERYONE: Amene!

Tau, Kala and Tonga all run towards the food. The minister puts his hand out to stop the boys.

MINISTER: Ahha! Why is it that every time we have a Niuean feast, everyone runs to the table like we don't have food on this Island? There is plenty of food for everyone, but you all want to rush to the food. As the minister of the Hakemai e Maama Church I declare all the food on the table, including the peka, mine. Take it to the car.

AUNTY: The bat is for Fili.

MINISTER: The bat is for me. Take it to the car.

The boys protest over the minister taking the food.

MINISTER: Children of the world, please stop the fighting. The lesson for today is 'Mama mo Pepa, tiaki e la tau . . .'

Tau, Aunty Leta, Kala and Tonga reply with a song.

AUNTY/TAU/KALA/TONGA: 'Ka latau a mua fanogonogo fanau.'

MINISTER: 'Kua ita mama toto e kato leta.'

TAU/KALA/TONGA: 'Mavehe, Mavehe fano hane fai.'

The minister is not happy.

MINISTER: Not right. Who wrote those words – if Mama goes and don't come back? Who's going to look after her savage children? She must return back home to look after you kids. Liu foki!

Everyone sings the song with the actions.

AUNTY/TAU/KALA/TONGA: 'Mama mo Papa. Mama mo papa tiaki e la tau, ka latau a mua, fanogonogo e fanau. Kua ita a mama toto e kato leta . . . fano, fano ti liu mai . . .'

MINISTER: Haia!

The minister exits. Aunty stands with the boys, waving to the church minister. They sing the song again but change the ending, making a mockery of the minister as a fake preacher.

EVERYONE: 'Fano, fano akoako fakavai!'

They all stand looking at the empty table.

TONGA: I could eat a horse!

They all laugh.

AUNTY: Go and find something for dinner. I don't care what you boys get.

Tau, Kala and Tonga exit.

AUNTY: Very sorry about that Fili.

FILI: I'm not hungry anymore. So, where do I sleep?

Aunty Leta points to his feet.

AUNTY: Where you are standing.

FILI: Right here? Isn't this the kitchen?

AUNTY: Yes, but now it's your bedroom.

FILI: Where do the boys sleep?

AUNTY: Up the tree.

FILI: Up the tree?

AUNTY: Just jokes. They sleep at the back.

FILI: I thought I'd be sleeping at my family house.

AUNTY: No one has slept in your family house since your parents left for New Zealand. You'll be fine here. Listen, if you hear noise at night, it just a ghost!

FILI: Are you for real? Serious?

AUNTY: I thought you were in a gang?

FILI: Yeah, I'm in a gang, but only part time gangster, Aunty.

Aunty laughs.

AUNTY: Goodnight. Koe kia.

FILI: Yep. Koe kia.

Aunty Leta exits. Fili finally gets time to himself. He checks his phone. He tries to ring out but the phone isn't working.

Scene 4

A guitar is heard offstage. Enter ELAVISI, a flamboyant character dressed in blue Hawaiian shirt with white pants. He's the singer on the Island. He strums his guitar. It's the same actor who played the church minister.

FILI: Who are you?

ELAVISI: I'm your next-door neighbour, ma bro!

FILI: Hey, aren't you the minister?

ELAVISI: Niue is a small place. We all look the same around here. My name is Elavisi.

FILI: Okay. So what do you want?

ELAVISI: I'm your friend, my bro. No need to be so harsh. Welcome home, Fili.

FILI: You know me?

ELAVISI: Everyone knows you, ma Fili G!

FILI: How do you know my name? The old lady told you?

ELAVISI: G Fili, my Fili.

FILI: Hey, only those in my circle call me that! How do you know my name G?

ELAVISI: Pule na koe. So . . . you got anything for me?

Elavisi puts his hand out.

FILI: For what, my Nika?

ELAVISI: For bring your bed, ma tiko!

FILI: My bed? Cool. Where's my bed?

ELAVISI: Coming, my Nika, but first you gotta pay da man.

FILI: How much do you want?

ELAVISI: Whatever is in your pocket.

FILI: Two fifty.

ELAVISI: Two hundred and fifty dollar? Sweet.

FILI: Sweet. Two dollar fifty!

Fili reaches into his pocket and takes out two dollars fifty and gives it to Elavisi.

ELAVISI: Kili fusi!

FILI: What does that mean?

ELAVISI: It means, I'll take your watch too.

FILI: My watch? It's a gift from my girl.

ELAVISI: I'm sure she's rich. Come on, do you want your bed or not?

Fili hands over his wristwatch.

FILI: I really don't know you, but you better not be a trickster.

ELAVISI: Trick or treat, here we come. Thanks, ma bro. [Calling offstage.] Bring his bed, ma tau keis!

Tau and Tonga enter dressed in traditional Niuean costume, wearing beautiful leis around their necks. They bring on a bed mattress, a pillow and a drinking coconut for Fili. Elavisi plays the guitar and sings a love song for Fili.

ELAVISI: 'Mohe au ne po, ti miti au kia koe kapitiga; kae poi mai na koe moe toto, toto haaku lima; mo ha ni, mo ha ni e tau manatu oti, e tau manatu oti; kae mua atu ni haaku miti, ne miti kia koe oi eaa, agi mai e matagi mo e manogi, e tau fiti lagakali; fuluhi fano au, fuluhi fano au ke he fonua, ke fonua kae mohe alafiha ai au, he po katoa.'

Fili starts to doze off. Elavisi stands over Fili playing his guitar. Fili wakes up in a fright.

FILI: What you doing?

Elavisi changes his song. Fili goes back to sleep and Elavisi continues to play his song to the audience.

ELAVISI: Love me, piri, fakaalofa mai kia au; kua kikila haau a tau mata tuga e tau pusi ne kali; kapapola he falepuga; Love me, ma haaku moka; haaku fisi kaute; kua fifigo tei a koe tuga e tau Maoli ne mokulu e tau nifo he maaga ko Otala; kua fano fai au, neke ko e tau kuli; ai fia nofo au i Fonuakula.

Elavisi runs offstage. Lights fade to dark blue with the moon shining on Fili. He dreams in his sleep.

Scene 5

The dream is a mixture of Niuean traditional dance and European-style comedy. The lights are flashing like it's a disco but you can still see the action onstage. The song playing is 'Poi Poi' by Napoleon Manetoa. It tells the story of Captain James Cook's first attempt to land his ship on Niue Island only to be chased by the Islanders. James Cook later gave Niue the name 'Savage Island'.

In his dream, Fili G is being chased. He runs to all corners of the stage only to be chased onstage by his ancestors. When they finally catch up to him they hold him up, offering the boy as a sacrifice.

Aunty Leta enters, waving a meat cleaver towards Fili. The dream turns into a nightmare as Fili realises what's going to happen. He tries to escape but the savages hold him down as Aunty Leta walks towards him with the cleaver. The savages pull his pants down to his undies. Just as the cleaver falls between his legs, the lights go out!

Scene 6

Fili wakes to find Aunty Leta and Tau, Kala and Tonga (shirtless) laughing like little kids. The boys point to the mattress. Fili's nightmare has made him wet the mattress. Aunty throws a pair of shorts at him.

AUNTY: You'll need these. Take the mattress out to dry.

Kala and Tonga drag the mattress offstage. Fili quickly changes into the shorts. The boys look on.

AUNTY: Don't tease the boy. Only I can, kia?

TAU: OK, ma aunty.

AUNTY: I'm just heading out to town to get some breakfast. Anybody need any coconuts?

Aunty laughs to herself. She exits.

TAU: Bro! Do you know a guy in Mangere called Billy?

FILI: Billy who?

TAU/KALA/TONGA: PILITOME!

FILI: Who's Pilitome?

TAU/KALA/TONGA: Not you! No cut. No good.

Tau starts the PILITOME song, mocking Filimoana.

TAU: 'Ai la pilitome, ai la pilitome ... Ko e hele ha ne fai, ko e hele ha ne fai.'

The boys run offstage. Fili remains onstage. He doesn't know what the big deal is. He looks down and realises why they were teasing him. He's not been circumcised.

FILI (calling offstage): Pilitome! Right, I see now. Yeah, I'm laughing with you guys now! Bloody savages! Yeah, go on and tell everyone about it. I'm not ashamed. I really don't understand the big deal about getting it cut.

The boys run back onstage, still singing the PILITOME song. Fili tries to hide but there is nowhere to hide. He dances and tries to sing with them. The boys run offstage again. Fili turns to the audience.

FILI: Really? I mean, it's *my* dingaling! I can do whatever I want with it. These savages calling me Filitome! Foreskin! Foreskin! Kilifusi!

The boys come back onstage doing the Kilifusi dance.

TAU/KALA/TONGA: Kilifuti, Kilifuti ulu Sihamani!

Tau, Kala and Tonga run offstage again. Filimoana has had enough of the games. He calls out to them.

FILI: I really don't care, mate! I hate this island anyway!

Filimoana finds himself alone. He's frustrated. He just wants to go home.

Scene 7

Footsteps are heard offstage. Enter GRANDFATHER, the ghost of Peniamina, Fili's great-great-grandfather, dressed in white and walking with a walking stick. The character is played by the same actor who played Elavisi.

GRANDFATHER: Thieves, robbers – ko hai ne fakaofofo a au? Who awoke me? . . . Who are you?

FILI: Can people stop sneaking up on me?

GRANDFATHER: You hiding from the boys of the village? You afraid of those village idiots?

FILI: I'm not afraid! I'm just . . . tired. Tired of . . . everyone here . . .

GRANDFATHER: You are new here – I can tell. What is your name?

FILI: Does everyone work for the police here or something? Everywhere I go on this island – everyone asks the same questions – 'What is your name? Who are your parents?'

GRANDFATHER: Your name!

FILI: Fili G!

GRANDFATHER: Your Niuean name?

FILI: OK! Man, you sound just like my old man – always demanding an answer! My name is Filimoana Peniamina. Happy now?

GRANDFATHER: Pine loa hakemai e maama Maka Fitu?

FILI: Yeah. Maka Fitu. And I'm related to Peniamina. The guy who brought the gospel to Niue. Happy now, old man? And who are you?

GRANDFATHER: Finally the son of Mutalau has returned. Kua liu mai tei e tama tokaveli, tama fuata toa lekaleka. Hola mai he tau matua kelea ne nonofo he motu mamao ko Aotearoa. Ai malika mai taha, ai ua, ai tolu, ke hau ke fakafeleveia mo e ha lautolu a matua Aala mai! Aala mai ma tau tupua! Kua kikila mai e maama ke he motu fakahelehele ha tautolu ko Niue Fekai Nukutuha matamaka he Pasifika.

FILI: Are you a ghost?

GRANDFATHER: Boohoooo!

FILI: Oh shit! What's the matter with people on this island? Can I just talk to some normal people?

GRANDFATHER: I am your great-great-great-great-grandfather. From the line of Nukai Peniamina ne tahake mai e maama ki Niue Fekai kae fakapouli he matafatata he siale!

FILI: Damn, that's deep! What is that in English, old man?

GRANDFATHER: Your parents ran away from this place.

FILI: They didn't run away.

GRANDFATHER: Yes! They ran away.

FILI: They did not run away.

GRANDFATHER: Keep sticking up for your parents. Go on. Run away! Just like the rest of them.

FILI: They didn't run away. The went with the cultural group in . . .

GRANDFATHER: And never returned . . . you think I don't know that?

FILI: Looking around here there is nothing for my parents – what you want them to come back to? Some coconut trees and empty houses?

GRANDFATHER: These houses were not empty once upon a time – it was full of life. Your parents. They made a promise that they will look after our house. Look after our home.

FILI: My mother came back a few years ago.

GRANDFATHER: And she just stood outside the house. Go back home. There is nothing here for you.

FILI: What you want them to do – dig your grave and take you with them?

GRANDFATHER: Tau manu he lagi, tau ika I tahi, afa mai, afa mai! Ia ha ha!

In fear, Filimoana, runs offstage.

Scene 8

Kala, Tau and Tonga run on and offstage, calling and searching for a pig. Kala comes onstage huffing and puffing.

KALA: Yup! Yup! Yup!

Kala runs offstage. Tonga runs onstage.

TONGA: Yup! Yup! Yup! (Runs offstage.)

Fili, tired and exhausted, runs onstage.

FILI: Can someone please tell me what's going on? They told me to go and feed the pig and next thing I know the pig is out!

Tau runs onstage with a knife. He's mad at Filimoana.

TAU: PILITOME! Why did you let the pig go?

FILI: I didn't let the pig go!

TAU: Yes you did! Don't just stand there – you go that way and I'll meet you on the other side. Go! Go!

Both run offstage. Tonga comes back onstage, calling for the boys in Tongan.

TONGA (in Tongan): Where are you guys?

Tau comes running back onstage.

TAU: Tonga! How many times I told about your horse language? That's why everyone here is confused! Go that way . . . hurry!

Both run offstage. Fili comes running back onstage, meeting Kala.

KALA: Why did you let the pig go, Pilitome?

FILI: I didn't let the pig go! It just took off. You guys got lots of pigs.

KALA: That's the one that Aunty wants for dinner! You go that way and I go this way!

Kala runs offstage. Filimoana stays onstage.

FILI: We been running for over an hour to chase one pig. Really don't want to run anymore, but I don't want to let these guys down.

Tau runs back onstage.

TAU: Are you tired, Pilitome?

FILI: No!

TAU: Yes, you are. OK. If the puaka comes this way, you tackle it!

FILI: Like tackle the puaka?

TAU: You scared?

FILI: No!

TAU: Tackle the puaka or I'll pilitome you right here!

FILI: Okay, I'll hold it.

TAU: Yeah, OK, hold it for the Pilitome, ka ma Fili G!

FILI: No! I'll hold the pig.

TAU: Good. Hold the pig and not your futi hula hula.

Tau runs off, leaving Filimoana onstage.

FILI: I really want to go home now. Shit! Damn! So many bloody mosquitoes!

TAU (offstage): Puaka!

The pig runs onstage and confronts Filimoana. The pig runs offstage.

FILI: Guys, the pig!

Tonga comes onstage.

TONGA: Good one – just stand there like a girl. Which way did the pig go?

Filimoana points in a random direction. Tonga goes after the pig.

TONGA/TAU (from offstage): Fili, the puaka!

Tau and Kala back onstage.

TAU/KALA: Did you see the pig?

FILI: That way.

The boys chase the pig offstage but the pig turns and comes back onstage. Filiomana screams.

FILI: The pig is here!

Tau and Kala arrive onstage. They see the pig.

TAU: Tackle the pig!

Fili closes his eyes and tackles the pig, but misses. The pig runs offstage. Tau is disappointed.

TAU (to audience): And that's why Niue doesn't have a professional rugby team!

FILI: I tried.

TAU: Not good enough.

Tonga walks onstage like a boss carrying the tied-up pig. He throws the pig towards Filimoana's feet.

TONGA: He's lying – I saw him just stand there talking to himself and the puaka ran past him. He was scared!

FILI: I was not scared.

TONGA: What were you doing then?

FILI: I was praying.

TONGA: What a lying horse! Anyway, here is the pig. It takes a Tongan to catch this beast! [He turns to the audience.] You see, this pig was smart but not smart enough for Tonga. It tried to hide but when it saw me it ran. I climbed up the mango tree and waited for it to come back. I just like a Ninja flying through the air but somehow the pig ran off. He saw the pig, but just stood there like a girl waiting for his bus. When the pig came back my way, I knew I had no choice but to take it head on. The pig saw me – it's eyes were angry like the hungry shark. We both looked into each other's eyes. I say to the pig, 'It's time to go home, Babe'. The pig charge at me. Oh, shit the pig gonna run it straight. Okay, piggy, piggy, come to your daddy. Boom! I shoulder-charge Babe straight on its flat nose. The pig goes down and out for the eight count! And we have a NEW champion of Niue – the kid from Tonga!

Kala applauds Tonga. Tau smiles. Filimoana cheers.

TAU: What a build-up guy. Why you happy for? The pig is yours.

Tau hands the knife over to Filimoana.

FILI: What you want me to do with the pig? Take the pig back to Aunty?

TAU: Yep. Take the pig back to Aunty. Dead. She wants the pig dead. Tamate e puaka.

KALA: Hey, it will make you a man.

FILI: How does killing a pig make me a man?

TAU: Oh well, cut your pilitome then!

Fili is furious and turns the knife towards Tau.

FILI: No more! No more jokes about me!

TAU: Haia! Now he's angry. Good boy, Pilitome. Kill the pig. Vave!

Filimoana has got no choice but to kill the pig. He slowly walks towards the pig. He stops and turns to the audience.

FILI: How does it prove my manhood if I kill this animal? I want to tell them that I'm not strong – that I don't have the heart to do it. Scream to the world that I don't have the strength to kill. Give me something else to kill – like an ant or a fly on a wall – but not a pig.

TAU: Hurry up, Pilitome, the pig is waiting!

FILI: To kill, to end his life, to feed us all – the poor beast. [Fili breaks down and cries. Looks for support from the boys and gets none.] Why? Why does it have to be like this? This poor animal's life in my hands. Today is the last day, the last hour, the last second of his life is now. Farewell, piglet.

TAU: Haia ma puaka mafola e fenoga!

FILI: Farewell, baby!

TAU/KALA/TONGA: Haia ma baby!

Filimoana becomes dramatic, over the top, like a character from Shakespeare.

FILI: To take a life, to end it, it's the end for the pig and I who will end his life. I free you today, pig. Your death is not the end but rather a start to your journey.

TAU: Hurry up, Shakespeare! The pig is not going to answer you back with all the praying! Vave!

Filimoana screams and the boys echo back his screams.

TAU: Hurry up, crybaby!

Filimoana raises the knife to the pig. He slowly circles the pig. The light changes to red. All eyes are on Filiomona. The boys, in a circle, start the chant, whispering and encouraging Filimoana.

TAU/KALA/TONGA (chanting): Tu te ma mea ke koli ha kua puni maala he to; Hapa pu hapa pa hapa pu hapa pa; Liti a Lafaia, hi ha hi ha; Liti a Lafaia, hi ha hi ha; Talali talali fakapaea ki Pakulaa, talali; talali fakapaea ki Pakulaa; Pulou, pulou, pulou a nou; HI!!!

Filimoana drives the knife into the pig. Filimoana falls to his knees. He looks up to the sky.

FILI: I have blood on my hands. My hands have blood. Stains that will last for ever. Oh, Lord, I have sinned.

KALA: Haia ma toa. You're man now.

TONGA: When the pig is out of the umu, you going to enjoy the taste of the puaka.

TAU: Tonga, clean the pig and take it back with us. [Picks the knife up.] You coming, Fili?

FILI: I'll walk back. I know my way.

TAU: Filimoana, you did good today. [He takes the knife, wipes the blood off with his shirt. He places the knife on Fili's head.] Rise FILIMO ANA PENIAMAI son of MAKAFITU. Welcome home, son of Mutalau!

Tau walks offstage.

Scene 9

Footsteps are heard from a distance. The voice of Grandfather is calling out to Fili.

GRANDFATHER: Stand up, son of Peniamina.

Grandfather arrives onstage.

FILI: I can't. I just killed a pig.

GRANDFATHER: You killed a pig, and now you can't stand up? It's only a pig. They need it to feed the village.

FILI: I'm just tired. Tired of everyone here. Tired of everyone picking on me.

GRANDFATHER: I thought you were Fili G?

FILI: At home I'm Fili G. I'm trying to be strong here. I just don't fit into this place. I can't wait to go back home.

GRANDFATHER: You can't live in this place overnight. You need to come back and learn the ways.

FILI: What ways? The Niuean ways? There is nothing here for me.

GRANDFATHER: There is your family home.

FILI: My family home is in Mangere!

GRANDFATHER: And who owns that land? Who owns that house? Get up. Your time is up. Go back home then, but you must return. This is your home, ma Fili – everything here is yours. This is your land. This is our home. This Fonua. This land, Niue Fekai has always been a place of our hearts.

FILI: It's great to be home, Granddad. I don't know when I'll be back – but I promise I'll clean your headstone before I go.

GRANDFATHER: Fakaaue lahi la ma mea. Filimoana, I bless you, my son, with all the knowledge of this land. May you use it to bring our people back home. For here is where we need them, here is where they will learn the ways of the old and embrace the knowledge of our people.

Grandfather chants 'Kai tagata'.

GRANDFATHER: 'Ko mautolu nei ko e tau tagata kai tagata . . .'

Filimona catches on to the chant.

FILI: I have so much to learn.

GRANDFATHER: It's your want to learn. Your want to embrace the ways of the Kai tagata.

FILI: I'll try my very best to learn.

GRANDFATHER: Not only for you, but for the generations to come. I forgive your parents too. Tell your mother the next time . . .

FILI: To come inside the house.

GRANDFATHER: Good boy.

FILI: I also want to clean up the house. Rebuild it. It's our family home.

GRANDFATHER: That's up to you, my son. Tell your father when his time is up – come and rest beside us for here is where his fonua was buried and here is where he belongs.

FILI: I'll tell him that.

GRANDFATHER: And one more thing . . . get it cut!

FILI: What! You mean . . . ? But it's not our ways. It was brought to us by the missionary to get it cut.

GRANDFATHER: Okay. It's your choice – Fili-tome.

FILI: Filitome! That's a good one, Granddad. I love you. You take care.

GRANDFATHER: I'll be waiting for you when your time is up.

Filimoana watches his grandfather with tears. Grandfather starts the song, a farewell song. They both sing it to each other before separating.

FILI/GRANDFATHER: Ko e lalolagi lahi ia hana,
Ti fakaenene ho manatu kia ai
Kua eke mo puna ke tafe mai
E malaia
Tafe mai e malaia
Haga mai la ke lali a taua
He mai mouiaga fiafia
Kua humelie loto
He pulotu he lima.

Aunty Leta walks onstage singing the same song, carrying a bowl of water. She places the water next to Fili. Fili washes his face and hands. Tau brings on a brand new shirt. Kala gives him his bag. Tonga gives Fili a necklace. They all sing the song together. Fili changes. He looks clean and new. The family all take seats. Filimoana stands. He reaches into his bag and gets his notebook out.

FILI: I don't have anything to give you all. All I have is words. I am a poet. I have written a poem for all of youse. [He opens the book and reads the poem.] It's in my blood to be Niuean. I am guided by my ancestors – I am walking with the ghost of my grandfather. From the great line of Nukai Peniamina ne tahake mai e maama ki Niue Fekai, he is guiding me. I am fearless for I have found me. Everything about me is Niuean. I didn't see it or want it in the first place and now I am loving it. My DNA is pure Niueanness. Everything – my hair, my skin, my lips, my spirit, my heart – is Niuean.

[He closes his book and continues reciting his poem.]

Everything, from my roots to my soul, is Niuean, from this earth that I stand on, the ground that I walk on, every step towards the future guided by the hula of my family – from my village of Mutalau Ululauta ne hakemai e maama to this fonua that my forefathers walked on, before me and before them. I am home. Mata ki luga ma Niue.

Aunty Leta gives Fili a hug.

AUNTY: Hope you come back soon.

FILI: I will, Aunty.

KALA/TONGA/TAU: Can you bring us some chocolate and some . . .

AUNTY: Ua ho ha! He's going to miss his flight.

FILI: Can you guys start on my family house? I'll send the money from New Zealand.

AUNTY: Are you sure? They all laugh.

FILI: It's a promise.

AUNTY: We will look after it as we have done through the years. Love to your parents.

TAU: When you come back your house going to be high like a building!

KALA: High like the Sky City casino!

TONGA: And higher like palace of King Tupou . . .

AUNTY: Hoha!

Tonga runs up to Filimoana. Everyone is listening in on the conversation.

TONGA: Toko, if you can look for my family in Otahuhu.

FILI: Otahuhu is big place. How will I find your family?

TONGA: I'm related to all the Tongans in Otahuhu. You will find them. Tell them I'm getting married. I'll get a passport and then I'm off to New Zealand.

AUNTY: Who you getting married to, Kai nua?

TAU/KALA: You found a girl? Where?

TONGA: The village of Vaiea! A few new girls have just arrived from Tuvalu. [Tonga starts to sing.] 'Good bye Mutalau. We off to ama uga, ama uga I Vaiea.'

TONGA/TAU/KALA: 'Taufifine fuluola ne o mai i Tuvalu. O fai a tautolu e tau fuata tolopo! Siooohhhheeeee!'

The boys march offstage like soldiers.

AUNTY: Come back here! Fia kalaga he ha? Where you guys going?

The boys argue with their aunty.

FILI (calling to them): Ah, family! I gotta go now.

TAU: Haia ma Filimoana!

FILI: Haia ma Tauhemaka!

KALA: To fele!

FILI: Ai mavehe!

Elavisi enters to say goodbye.

ELAVISI: Koe ma Fili.

FILI: Haia ma Toa!

AUNTY: Koe ma son.

FILI: Mata ki luga . . . monu . . . monu.

EVERYONE: Monu . . . monu Tagaloa!

Elavisi plays the guitar and everyone sings – Niu Silani mo Niue . . .

FILI: Haia ma tau keis!

EVERYONE: Ae ae – haia ma – PILITOME!

Lights snaps out to black. The original track of 'Niu Silani mo Niue' is playing in the dark.

The End

SAI Ē REUNION
LOLO FONUA

Sai ē Reunion

Written by Lolo Fonua

With creative input from Loma Teisi and `Una Fūnaki

About the author
Siulolo (Lolo) Fonua is a New Zealand-born Tongan raised on the west side of Auckland. She graduated from the Pacific Institute of Performing Arts in 2011. Lolo wrote her first Tongan play *Sai ē Reunion* in 2013 and directed and staged it that same year. She took the show to Sydney in 2014, where it was performed at Riverside Theatre. Lolo also co-wrote (with Lauren Jackson) the theatre play *Lollywitch of Mumuland*, commissioned by Auckland Theatre Company in 2015. Lolo is the founder of LFP (Lolo Fonua Productions) and is the creator of *Free Katas*, a Tongan comedy web series. She wrote, produced, directed and edited the first two seasons, which have gone viral in the Tongan community. Lolo continues to create new Tongan shows both through theatre and in film.

Synopsis
Mele, born and raised in Tonga, is a typical good Christian girl who longs for a better life in New Zealand. Mele comes to Auckland for a family reunion and meets up with her two crazy cousins who teach her how to live, laugh and love.

Dedication
To my parents, Paula and Mafi Fonua, for always without fail supporting me and my dreams.
    I love you and thank you.
    Ko e `Otua mo Tonga ko hoku tofi`a.

Acknowledgements

Lauren Jackson, Olivia Taouma, Lima Production Writers' Workshop, Louise Tu'u, 'Una Fūnaki, Loma Teisi, Leki Jackson-Bourke, Shauntelle Jones, Losa Tui, Samson Salu, Paula Mohenoa, 'Aisea Lātū, Nastasia Wolfgramm, Jase Manumu'a, Mark De Jong, Bob Savea, Maile Fīnau, Lyncia Muller, KC Meyers, Tongan Creative Collective, Alison Quigan, Mangere Arts Centre, Kaufo'ou Fonua, Talanoa and Trevor Raine, Senituli Fonua, John Fonua and family, Vita Vaka, 'Amanaki Prescott-Faletua, Mario Faumui, Stuart Hoar, Playmarket New Zealand, Pipa, Sean Coyle, Letti Chadwick, Tweddi Waititi, Anapela Polavatia, OMAC, Sau e Siva, Lōloa and Sio 'Alatini, Gerard Cronin, Emma Lūtui, Manukau District Court, Tagata Pasifika, Riverside Theatre, 'Ana Moala and family, Pasifiki Lounge, Mele Young, Malita 'Ofamo'oni and my extended family.

First performance

Sai ē Reunion premiered in 2013 at Mangere Arts Centre, Auckland, and was produced by Sai ē Productions.

Cast

MELE: Loma Teisi
LOTE/AUNTY SI'I: Losa Tui
PETI: Shauntelle Jones
AUNTY LAHI: 'Una Fūnaki
ROGER WRITE/DEVIL: Leki Jackson-Bourke
DIRECTOR: Siulolo Fonua

Characters

MELE: 18, born and raised in Tonga, first time to New Zealand, good girl, always does what she is told. Loves God, church and family. Is respectful, kind and innocent. English is her second language.

LOTE: 20, New Zealand-born Tongan. Oldest of the cousins, with strong motherly instincts. Smart – she is at university studying medicine. She secretly likes to party, smoke and drink alcohol.

PETI: 19, biggest of the cousins, loves to eat, very cheeky and loud. She is close with Lote, and also secretly likes to party, smoke and drink alcohol.

AUNTY LAHI: Queen of the family, highly revered by her nieces and everyone. She is big, strong, funny and loud. She loves the church but is known to use bad language sometimes.

AUNTY SI'I: Sidekick to Aunty Lahi, but more sensible and righteous.

ROGER WRITE: Supervisor at the onion farm. In his 40s. He is kind and friendly with a secret that will surprise.

FAIFEKAU VOICE-OVER: Minister's voice.

DEVIL: Resides in Hell. Energetic, spooky and animated. Wears a black cape.

Sai ē Reunion

Scene 1: Welcome to New Zealand

Darkness. Song – Mr Bean theme – plays. Spotlight slowly appears middle of empty stage. Music fades to end. Sound effect: Plane landing, spotlight fades away.

VOICE-OVER: Mālō lelei. Flight 139, Royal Tongan Airlines, from the friendly island of Tonga has just arrived in Aotearoa, New Zealand. We hope you enjoy your stay. Thank you.

Song – 'Lome Lome' remix. Lights up. AUNTY LAHI and AUNTY SI'I enter. They walk around, unsure where to find the Arrivals area. MELE nervously walks out. The aunties wave at Mele and start heading towards her. Mele approaches them and the aunties walk straight past her and accidentally greet someone random. Finally, Mele gets their attention and they greet and hug.

LAHI: Hauē, feti feti.

SI'I: Hauē, sio atu ki he fo'i talavou` . . . sio ki hono fo'i va'e`, fo'i ta'ahine Tonga mo'oni . . . Ko ho ta'u fiha eni?

MELE: Ta'u taha-valu.

SI'I: Ewweee!

LAHI: Fēfē atu 'a Ngalu mo Kaufusi?

MELE: 'Io 'oku sai pē 'a Ngalu mo Kaufusi, 'oku ngāue 'a Ngalu . . . 'i he.

SI'I: Sai ā, 'ai ke ta ō ki 'api, 'oku tali mai e kau folau, vave.

Aunties start to walk.

MELE: Aunty! Fie kai Mekitōnolo.

SI`I: Si`i, fa`a kai . . . `io ta ō drive thru he Mekitōnolo, `o `omai ho geeze burga.

Dance sequence. 'Lome Lome' remix resumes. The girls do Tongan dance moves – getting into formation of car seating. Mele is so excited looking out. They arrive at McDonald's.

LAHI: Yes, gan I have three pig mak kombo pleas and a geezze burga. Thank ku and weh . . . make it upsize please.

They get their order and drive away. They arrive home.

SI`I: Mele! `Alu `o fe`iloaki mo [pointing to random people in the audience]. Mele, Lahi, mo Mele si`i, mo Mele Seini, ko Mele Sālati-paka, mo Mele faka`ofa . . .

LAHI: Mele, `alu `o ngaahi mai ha kapa tī?

Mele obeys Aunty Lahi.

SI`I: Mele, `alu `o fe`iloaki mo e Faifekau?

Mele stops. Obeys Aunty Si`i.

LAHI: Mele, `alu `o fufulu e peleti`?

Mele obeys Aunty Lahi.

LAHI/SI`I (both calling randomly and in different pitch voices): Mele, Mele, Mele, Mele . . .

Mele can't keep up . . . she falls to the ground.

LAHI/SI`I (softly together): Mele . . .

MELE: Hoi . . . [rolls her eyes].

LAHI: Pea hā, Mele? How many boyfriends you have?

MELE: Si`i, no boyfriend kuo` u lotu ma`u pē.

LAHI: Si`i tuku ho`o māhualoi . . . ke `ilo. When I was your age I was have one boyfriend at church . . . one in town and one where the bus stop is . . . Yes, I was vela vela and all the boys want me but I had to come to NZ with your grandpa and set up the church here and I just stay with Grandpa here and look after him. I have no one to date but lucky I was get my papers pea` u nofo ai pē i Niu Sila` ni.

MELE: Si`i, tuku ho`o loi. How many boyfriend you have here??

LAHI: Shhh!!! `Oku` ke fakamatalili mai kiate au! . . . `Oua! [Laughs.] Si`i, no boyfriend want me because I was get fat. That's why, Mele, you must look after your sino` and find a man now so when you eat the Mekitōnolo and KFC and get fat like me you still have a man, hē!!

MELE: Si`i, te u `alu pē ki he gym and `ai Zumba.

LAHI: `Ai ho pepa` ke ma`u, na`a ha`u e kau pōlisi `o `ave koe because you not get your paper pea` ke `alu `o lele ho bumbum ke slim down ke ke `asi talavou ki he sio mai e kakai`.

MELE: `Io fiema`u ke ma`u `eku pepa` ke u nofo heni `o ngāue mālohi ke fakafoki e pa`anga ke tokoni atu kia Mum 'n' dad `i Tonga.

LAHI: `Io poto, Mele. Ko ho `ofa mo e ngāue mālohi` `e Tāpuaki`i koe `e Sihova. Fanongo mai! Tapu ke ke `alu ki he Naiti Kalapu, `oua inu and smoke. When you wake up, wash face, brush teeth and put the lipisitiki on, pea ke `ai ho `ulu` ke faka`ofo`ofa, pea` ke fanongo ki he akonaki `a e Faifekau ehh!! Ko e mo`oni ko eni` . . . Lotu kia Sihova pea ke `ave ho worries ki ai` pea ke trust `i ai` . . . mahino? And make sure you wipe your bum too. Hēh!

MELE: `Io `io [laughs].

LAHI: `Io `io. You break the rules, I break you, OK? Remember, I am your dad's oldest sister and you must respect and listen to me. Go make me a cup of tea, right now.

Offstage LOTE knocks on door and enters.

LOTE: Hello, Aunty???

LAHI: Weh Sālote. `Io ha`u `o fe`iloaki mo ho cousin Mele.

Lote greets Aunty Lahi.

LOTE [smiling broadly]: Hi Mele.

They greet.

LAHI: Sio atu Mele kia Lote . . . You look good. Ko Lote eni` `oku study ki he toketā . . . `oku fēfē e ako? [Look at Lote, she's got a good figure. How is school?]

LOTE: Yes, school is good. A lot of study to do, but that's what Mum and Dad want . . . so, yeah!

LAHI: Mmm . . . study mālohi Lote ke `ilo`, ko koe pē `oku smart `i he fāmili, sio atu ki ho cousin Mele nofo pē `i Tonga `o talangofua ki hono ongo mātu`a`, ko e ako `i Tonga` `oku faka`ofa mo`oni sio ki ho mātu`a` na `alu `o ngāue mālohi, pea` ke `alu koe `o `ai ho ako` ke lava, pea` ke toki lava `o mānava lelei, `o ma`u ho pa`anga mo ho siana.

LOTE: OK, Aunty [doesn't really understand].

LAHI: `Io sai, mo talanoa ke mo maheni weh ko fē `a Peti?

LOTE: She said she is coming soon.

LAHI: Tell that one to find a man before she die of heart attack, and Sā`lote, you look after your cousin Mele. If anything happen to her te u haeua koe! Mahino ē! Mo look after ho cousin, eh!

Aunty Lahi exits.

LOTE: Hahaha, yes Aunty, of course I will look after her. [Looks around.] Wow, the house is clean. I guess you did all this? I mean, the house is always clean but now it's like 'I can see my reflection' clean.

Mele smiles and raises her eyebrows.

LOTE: Oh, you speak English???

Mele smiles.

LOTE: Um OK ... [Attempts Tongan.] Nake fakamui ae loki??

Mele smiles and laughs.

LOTE: Aww, shame she can't even understand my plastic Tongan [laughs] ... Hmm [Lote tries to ask questions by acting it out.] How was your flight here? What is it like in Tonga? Hot? [Looks at McDonald's rubbish.] Oh, you had some McDonald's?

Mele smiles and nods. Offstage, PETI knocks on door.

PETI: Hello ... Lote?

LOTE: Aww yes!! Mele ... meet your other cousin, Peti.

Peti enters with KFC bucket under one arm and a chicken drumstick in the other hand.

PETI: [Accidently walks past Mele.] Aww ... anymore McDonald's? I'm like so hungry. Hope you guys are full from the McDonald's, 'cos I don't feel like sharing my chicken. [Laughs and sits down to eat.]

LOTE: Peti! This is our cousin Mele from Tonga.

Peti jumps up.

PETI: Aww! The one we have heard so much about. 'Mele go church', 'Mele stay home', 'Mele no boyfriend'. [Laughs.]

Mele smiles and nods.

PETI: What? Mele can't speak English? [Looks at Lote.] She must think I'm a fat shit, eating all this.

LOTE: Umm . . . maybe she's too shy to speak English?

PETI: So, do we have to teach her English? How are we supposed to communicate? Because my Tongan is just as plastic as yours.

LOTE: Well, I tried to speak Tongan, but she didn't understand. I guess this would be a good chance for us to improve our Tongan.

PETI: Of course she won't understand your Tongan . . . it's like listening to the Royal Family talk. You need to come down and speak at our level. Watch this.

Mele laughs.

PETI: Pea hā fefine Tonga? . . . [can't think of Tongan words]. You like here in Niu Sila?

Mele smiles and laughs.

LOTE: Sai ē.

PETI: Well, since you are the scholar in the family, perhaps you can teach her English.

LOTE: Um, excuse me, I'm studying to be a doctor.

PETI: Eww, do you think you're better than us, ae? What? Too cool to help your cousin from Tonga speak English so she can find a better life here?

LOTE: Just calm lalo . . . what's up with you?

PETI: I am broke . . . I got no money and no job. Dad is hassling me to find one and I keep sending my CV to every job on findajob.com. But really, who wants to hire someone like me? I mean, just look at me [upset about her weight]. Ohh well, thank God for KFC. [Sighs and starts eating.]

LOTE: Things will get better, Peti. If you keep trying and don't give up.

PETI: Thanks, 'Dr Phil'. [Continues eating.]

Awkward silence. Peti busy eating, Mele smiling and Lote thinking. Yet they keep smiling at each other.

LOTE (to Peti): You need to watch your eating.

PETI: OK, are you 'Dr OZ' now? Just because you're studying to be a doctor, doesn't mean you can solve all the problems of the world, OK? Leave me alone. I'm depressed, OK?

LOTE: What if we ask Uncle Pila for a job? Mele, do you have your work visa? Papers?

Mele smiles. Lote sighs.

LOTE: That's alright, because you don't need a visa to work at the onion farm.

Mele has a big smile.

PETI: What? Ohh, hell no. I am not going back to those days. Working on the farm and smelling like onions. Hell, no!

LOTE: I know . . . but this is the only way we can get money and take Mele eva around New Zealand. Otherwise we gonna have no money for these holidays and eat, eat, eat and get fat, fat, fat and depressed. [Looks at Peti.]

PETI: Oh, you bitch.

Mele reacts with look of horror.

PETI: Mele! You know what that word means, eh? Aww, that's why you are shocked.

MELE (shakes her head): No.

PETI (teasing her): Aww, Mele knows only the swear words. I guess you're not a good girl anymore.

LOTE: Aww, Mele is a naughty girl.

Mele can't handle it. She walks upstage.

LOTE: Mele, it's alright, we were just joking.

PETI: It's all your fault.

LOTE: Why don't you give her some chicken? She might feel better.

PETI: Too late. It's all finished. [Licks her fingers.]

Lote and Peti exit. Spotlight appears. Mele bends down on her knees and prays.

MELE: Cod, forkive me, I know that word is bad but Cod kive me the gonfeedence, I am too shy to speak Englis because if I say somefing wrong they laugh at me. Pliss kive me strengff to be me. Amen.

Mele lies down to sleep.

Scene 2: Church

Alarm clock goes off. Mele jumps up in a panic, running around trying to find clothes, brushing her hair and putting lipstick on. Mele exits. Aunty Si`i enters and starts singing a Tongan hymn.

SI`I: `Io . . . Fakafeta`i `Eiki . . .

Aunty Lahi enters during the prayer.

SI`I: Fefine? Ko fē ho tatā?

LAHI: Weh `i he toileti?

SI`I: Mani ē! Me`a fakamā mo`oni.

Si`i and Lahi laugh hard. Mele enters with Aunty Lahi's hat and joins them.

FAIFEKAU VOICE-OVER: Tell the truth and shame the devil.

Aunties look up and nod.

EVERYONE: `Emeni.

Everyone files outside the church.

LAHI (loud voice to the whole congregation): This is my niece. She is come all the way from Tonga . . . sino lelei and she single too . . .

Si`i pulls Mele aside and starts gossiping.

SI`I: Mele, sio atu ki he siana ko ē [pointing to people in the crowd] fo`i tula` . . . he was like your Aunty Lahi.

MELE: But what happen?

SI'I: His hair was fall out, that's what happen. [They laugh.] Sio ki he fefine `oku tangutu `i hē . . . ko `ene ta`ahine`, `oku haua `atā `io . . . na`e talamai `e Sela na`e sio ki ia `i Lepuhā ko e hulo-hula` `io . . . mo e fefine ko ē, `io . . . sio ki hono kauleka`, `oku ta`e-sū, `io `alu `ene mātu`a `o spend the money `i he kasino`, pea ta`e kai e kauleka` mani, me`a ta`e `ofa mo`oni.

Aunty Lahi catches one of the boys starring at Mele.

LAHI: Mmm eh eh eh . . . mata`i-ngeli! `Oua toe sio mai ki he`eku ta`ahine` nau taa`i koe heh. If I catch you look over here to my niece, I will make you go blind ehh.

SI'I: Sai ā we just finish church tau ō ā ki `api `o kai `etau haka` . . . `io nau wake up early `o `ai `etau lū sipi` moe talo` chop suey lo`i hoosi` mo e puaka`, I hope that's enough.

They all exit.

Scene 3: Sunday feast

They all arrive home. Mele and Peti set up the food.

LAHI: Peti ha`u `o `ai tēpile`, `omai e me`akai . . . te u `alu`o fetongi.

PETI: Mmmm yumm. I'm, like, so hungry. You bless the food.

Mele prays purposely in English so they know she can speak English.

MELE: Cod bless the food and Peti for being here. Fank you, lord Amen.

Peti is speechless. Lote walks in.

LOTE: Aww yumm. My favourite lū sipi hipi hipi.

PETI (to Lote): I didn't see you at church.

LOTE: Sorry, 'holy one'. I slept in.

PETI: If you died today, you would go to hell, because you weren't at church.

LOTE: Sii, if you eat too much you will die too.

PETI: You missed 'smiley face' here speak English. She blessed the food. Next time, Mele, pray that Lote would be just as good as us and go to church.

LOTE: I missed one Sunday. Doesn't mean I'm going to hell, but Mele why you not speak English before?

MELE: I am too shy because I was come from Tonga, but you was born here and you speak better, but me live in Tonga no good. You might laugh at me, when I say somefing wrong . .

LOTE: Our Tongan is not very good either. So we both the same. You help our Tongan and we help your English and everything else.

PETI: Yeah, so when I go to Lepuhā [Tongan nightclub] I can chat up the Tongan guys there.

LOTE: And if you died there you would go to hell [laughs].

MELE: You two, stop!

PETI: Aww, think you're bad, cause you speak English now?

Lote gets a text from Uncle Pila.

LOTE: I have great news! We start work tomorrow, at the onion farm.

PETI: That's not great news. That's torture. When tomorrow?

LOTE: Yes, tomorrow at 6am . . . so go pack your mahis [undies] because we going to the farm to stay with Uncle Pila and come back for church on Sunday.

MELE [excited]: OK, yay, we go work and get the money.

LOTE: Oh yeah. Mele, me and Peti will show you this view we always go to at night. It's very beautiful.

MELE: OK.

The girls start packing their clothes.

Scene 4: Drink up at the view top

Song – 'Your Man' by Josh Turner. Dance sequence. The girls sing along and do a Cowboy-style line dance getting into formation of car seating. They arrive at the secret location: a view that shows Auckland at night. It's peaceful and quiet. (Hidden Sign 'CAREFUL ONCOMING TRUCK!) The girls cover Mele's eyes and lead her.

LOTE: OK, you can look now . . .

Mele looks out at the view and is amazed.

MELE: Hauē ma`a lahi! [Very beautiful!]

PETI: Ko e hā? Ma`a mahi! [What you say? Clean undies!]

Peti pulls out the alcohol from the bag.

LOTE: Buahahaha `oua! [Stop it!]

PETI: Yes, the view is very beautiful, ae.

LOTE: Look, Mele, that is the Sky Tower – where I use to work in an `ōfisi at the top.

PETI: Si`i, tuku ho`o loi . . . You never even been inside the Sky Tower! [Both laugh.]

LOTE: Look, Mele. You see the red building there? That's where Peti's boyfriend works.

PETI: Where?

LOTE: At KFC. [Lote and Mele laugh.]

PETI: Shhh! Longo ho ngutu.

Offers alcohol to Mele She refuses.

MELE: Hauē `oua . . . Aunty Lahi say no drinking and I have to respect her.

LOTE: Mmmhhmm . . . and she say no smoking too. [Pulls out a cigarette to smoke.]

MELE (shocked): Si`i kotalī! . . . Do you not have respect for your aunty?

PETI: Ko e hā?

MELE: Do you know about the 'Mehikitanga'? Your dad's oldest sister? For us that is Aunty Lahi. She is the tallest in the family.

LOTE: You mean 'highest'? She's the highest rank in the family.

MELE: Yes, yes, whatever she say – that is the way. There is no other way . . . and the brother – who is my dad – must listen and respect Aunty Lahi whatever she say. And we must obey her. And if she finds you drink and smoke, she can fusi`i ho `ulu` ke homo . . .

PETI: Haue fakaoferrr . . . Is that why she gave Mona, our other cousin, a hiding?

LOTE (to Mele): You better not tell Aunty about us up here, drinking.

PETI: Yeah, you better keep your mouth shut, because your parents sent you here to work. Not to have fun, but to work every day, OK?

MELE (scared): OK.

PETI: That's all you are good for.

LOTE: Peti, you are killing the buzz.

PETI: She needs to know who is boss. So, Mele, you got a boyfriend? Or girlfriend? I know you, so don't come around here with your innocent act. I know if I put oil on you it will dry up.

MELE (smiles): If I put oil in your mouth, you die.

Lote laughs.

PETI: Buahaha. Miss Tonga got some jokes.

They all laugh.

LOTE: So, Mele, I'm going to ask you a question. Do you have a boyfriend?

MELE: No.

PETI: Like . . . ever?

MELE: No.

LOTE: Why?

MELE: Because I'm still kota – too young. I don't want to be a housewife and follow the man's everywhere he go in the church. Be a slave and cook breakfast, lunch, dinner. I want to be single and travel. That's why I here. Better to work, have fun, before rush to marry and not in love. No good.

LOTE: That is good, Mele. So when do you think you will get married?

MELE: 30 years.

PETI: You mean 30 years from now? Or when you turn 30?

LOTE: But what if you meet a guy here and he is the 'right one' and he asked you to marry him?

MELE: No. I only here to get my visa and work. Send the money back to Tonga. No boyfriends.

LOTE: 'Nek minit' you get married [laughs]. But how would you know if the guy is right?

MELE: I just look at him and know [dreamy eyes] . . . 'You are the one.' What about you?

LOTE: I had a boyfriend, but it just didn't work out [starts to cry]. So I'm still heartbroken . . .

PETI: Well! What I look for is someone who can lift me off my feet and just . . . well . . . I will keep the rest to myself.

LOTE: But it's about the personality and not the look, eh guys?

PETI: I don't know about you two but he gotta look good!

MELE: Si`i laupisi.

LOTE (looks at phone): OMG, we have to go now! It's a long drive.

PETI: Hauē faka`ofa.

The girls exit.

Scene 5: Working at the factory

Sound effect – factory background noises. Girls arrive. Tired and hungover. Their job is to pick out the rotten onions and throw them in the bin. Peti is just picking any onion, Lote doesn't want to get her nails dirty but Mele works hard and does it right. Behind them the supervisor is checking their work. He is unsure about Peti and Lote but is very happy with Mele. He smiles at Mele but she looks away. Sound effect – bells ring for smoko break. The girls come together.

LOTE: Haoue – did you see that guy staring at you? I think he likes you?

PETI: Aww I wish someone would like me.

MELE: I know someone who likes you.

PETI: Really? Who?

MELE: Jesus.

LOTE: Bahahaha tā ki ai. [Give me 'High Five'.]

MELE: Yeah, if you look in the Bible New Testament in 'John' . . .

LOTE: Mele! The joke ended at Jesus.

MELE: What? You say Jesus is a joke?

LOTE: Nooo! It's a joke so you stop after the laugh . . . Peti help me out here.

   ROGER enters.

ROGER: Hiii, you girls must be Pila's nieces?

GIRLS (smiling and being polite): Hiiiiiii.

ROGER: I'm Roger. Roger Write.

PETI: White?

ROGER (to Mele): No, Write, as in write on paper?

PETI: Aww, he didn't look at me while he was talking.

LOTE (to Peti): Si`i; (to Roger): Well, Roger, I'm Lote. This is Peti and this is Mele. So, how long you worked here?

ROGER: I've been here five years, just recently been made supervisor.

LOTE/PETI (teasing Mele): Aww . . . supervisor.

ROGER: Well, ladies, I better go. See you on the floor.

Roger exits.

LOTE/PETI (mocking Mele): Aww . . . 'see you on the floor'.

MELE (gets angry): Eww! No way!!

LOTE: OK! Take a chill pill, it's just a bit of fun. It's not serious – I mean, did you see him? [Laughs.]

Sound effect – bells ring signalling end of smoko break. Girls are back to work. Roger enters. He calls Mele to follow him to a new area to work.

ROGER: I really like your work, Meli [mispronounces Mele's name]. You will be working here from now on. It's much better. [They make eye contact.] Any questions?

Roger looks away (distracted by other things happening in factory).

Mele (to Roger): I don't like you!

Roger doesn't hear her but turns to Mele. She quickly smiles.

ROGER: You have a beautiful smile, Meli.

Roger exits. Mele stops smiling. Sound effect – bells ring signalling beginning of smoko break. Mele comes out to join the girls.

PETI: Aww, where did you go with your boyfriend??

MELE: He's not my boyfriend. He just show me what to do and I tell him, 'I don't like you.'

LOTE: Ko e hā?

MELE: But I think he was not listen.

PETI (jokingly): Girl, you need to pray and ask God to forgive you.

Mele gets scared and kneels down to pray.

LOTE (grabs Mele): No, Mele. Peti was joking. You just need to know the basics of 'When guy meets girl.'

MELE: Ko e hā?

PETI: Mele, when it comes to men, WE are the experts. Have you heard of the seven deadly signs of a man?

MELE: `Ika`i.

LOTE/PETI: Ko e hā?! What? Huh?

LOTE: You haven't heard of the 'seven deadly signs of a man'?

Peti and Lote look at each other and exchange a secret laugh.

LOTE/PETI: Tangutu.

PETI: If a guy is nice to you, disconnect any communication you have with him immediately.

LOTE: If a guy looks your way, then look into his eyes and give him the pūkana.

PETI: If a man asks you out to dinner you go and eat all the food and kai-fa'o and take some for your family.

LOTE: If a man tells you you're pretty, that normally means you're ugly so cry.

PETI: If he offers you a ride, scream out, 'Stranger, danger! Stranger danger!'

LOTE: If he touches you then you're gonna get pregnant.

PETI: If you fall for all of the above . . . then kill yourself.

Peti and Lote have serious faces and then burst out laughing (as they were just joking).

PETI: If you get to seven then all the men will be running after you just like me and Lote because we are single and lonely and unhappy.

LOTE: Eww . . . speak for yourself, Peti.

Lote and Mele laugh.

Scene 6: Girls just wanna have fun

Sound effect: bells ring, signalling that it's time to go back to work. Song: Cyndi Lauper – 'Girls Just Wanna Have Fun'. Montage without dialogue. Peti and Lote start dancing. They pull Mele along. She is hesitant at first, but joins in. Roger enters and the girls get back to work. Roger exits. The girls start mucking around again. This time Peti gets carried away and starts throwing the onions around and then jumps on the table to dance but does not notice Roger has reappeared behind her. The other girls notice Roger and get back to work. Finally, Peti turns and is shocked. Roger signals to Peti to get down and follow him to his office. They exit. Lote disappears. Mele is left by herself. Roger enters. They stare awkwardly at each other. Roger walks up to Mele, but she walks away from him. Roger exits. Spotlight appears on Mele.

MELE: Lord kive me strengff to resist the Tevil. My heart feels everywhere right now. I don't know what is happening and I don't know what is wrong with me. Please help me, Lord. Amen.

Scene 7: Find a man

At church. Mele enters and sits between Aunty Lahi and Aunty Si`i.

LAHI: Ko fē `a Lote mo hai?

SI`I: Mo Peti?

MELE: Ko naua ena `i tu`a.

SI`I: Poto `aupito, Mele, ho`o ha`u ki he lotu. Fēfē e ngāue?

MELE: Sai `aupito.

SI`I: Pea hā Mele? Koe hā e hingoa ho boyfriend?

MELE: `Ika`i.

LAHI: Eh? You wanna be single like me?

MELE: `Ika`i

LAHI: Weh, pea go find a man.

SI`I: `Oku hā ho Visa?

MELE: I'm wait for them to send the letter home. They say tis week. I hope I get my visa so I gan work, `eva ki he sky tower mo lepuhā.

LAHI (to Mele): `Oua nake kai hoku sū `ete.

MELE: Loi pe ia.

SI`I: Si`i, `e vave` ni pē ho`o `alu `o mali ē.

MELE: Si`i, tuku ia.

LAHI: Sio mai. I know some boys good for you, eh?

MELE: `Io ko hai?

LAHI: Ke `ilo `a Filimoto? Ko hono foha`.

SI`I: `Ika`i `oua. `Alu koe – marry a Pālangi, it make your life easy. If someone die in the family, they just have cup a tea then go home, you know? Go with the flow. But if you marry a Tongan it's no flow. It's send a pig, money, ngatu, ko e fakapiko atu.

LAHI: Si`i, `oku saiange pē Tonga`ia.

SI`I: Mele, your aunty want tamasi`i Tonga because of the koloa faka-tonga.

LAHI: Tuku ho`o kaimumu`a, `oku pau ange pē Tonga`, pea ke ma`u ho visa. Mahino Mele?

MELE: `Io.

SI`I: Sio mai`, mali pē koe, ke ma`u ho pepa` after. You can have divorce because then you already Kiwi koe tangata whenua koe . . . `ouaaa.

They all laugh. Aunty Lahi and Si`i stare at Mele.

MELE: `Io. Koe hā pē ho mo loto`, pea te u fai ki ai.

LAHI: `Io, sai.

Back into prayer.

SI`I/LAHI: `Io . . . mālō `Eiki! . . .

FAIFEKAU VOICE-OVER: Trust in the Lord and he will guide you. Amen.

LAHI/SI`I: Mālō mālō.

They exit.

Scene 8: Mele's visa

At home. Mele enters holding the visa letter.

MELE: Aunty koe tohi eni`.

LAHI: Mai ke u lau.

LAHI: Mele, I know it's not good news, eh? 'Thank you . . . for apply . . . for New Zealand citazen . . . Unfort . . . unfort . . . you did not meet all the require . . . ments . . . so your appli . . . cation . . . was denied.' Ohhh!!

Mele is sad.

LAHI: 'You must leave the country by the 23rd.' Weh . . . that is nek week. 'Monday 7am Pālangi time on Air New Zealand and must stay in Tonga for five years before you can apply to come back to NZ.' Hauē faka`ofa `a Mele! Ke `ilo . . . koe government ko `eni`, ko e ta`e`ofa mo`oni. Ko National Party `oku kovi . . . it's the devil . . . if you come in the time of Helen Clark you be citizen kkkk!! Me`a ta`e`ofa mo`oni a John Key ia . . .

Aunty Lahi exits. Spotlight appears. Mele, disappointed, stares out into space. She inhales and exhales, then exits.

Scene 9: Factory

Sound effect – bells ring, signalling time to go back to work. Lote and Peti know about Mele's situation. Mele enters and starts working hard right away.

LOTE/PETI: Are you alright? [Giving her the thumbs up.] Alright? [Smiling at her.] You alright?

Mele smiles and nods, but when they're not looking she frowns.

PETI: You should just stay here. Be an overstayer.

MELE: Noo! Because if they catch me they send me back to Tonga and I will never be allowed to come back.

LOTE: Yeah and you might bring shame on the family.

MELE: I have to go back because if not, then the immigration will not allow my parents to come, because I am haua here.

PETI: Well, do you want to go back?

MELE: Si`i – go back to what, hehh? Nothing in Tonga, only the same fing, wake up `ai the haka clean, clean, clean . . . eat, eat, eat and church, church, church. You lucky, you know. You live here and work 16 dola an hour. In Tonga, three dola an hour. But the food there [does ugly facials] is no good – too expenses. That's why the people go and stealing. Tonga is faka`ofa mo`oni. You lucky, Lote, study doctor. And you, Peti. Eat the KFC and Mekitōnolo . . .

PETI (daydreaming): I know . . . I know. [Snaps.] Hey!

LOTE: I have an idea. Why don't we find you a guy and you get married before Monday?

MELE: Si`i laupisi . . .

Mele walks backwards but still facing Lote and Peti.

MELE: It's alright, I will go.

Lote and Peti exit. Roger walks up behind Mele. Mele turns around and gasps with fright as she sees Roger and starts to faint. Roger quickly holds Mele and they slowly fall to the ground. Mele wakes up in the arms of Roger.

ROGER: Meli? Are you alright?

Mele stares at him.

MELE (soft voice): You are touching me.

ROGER: Yes, I am.

MELE: Seven deadly signs . . . [Mele jumps up]. If a man touches you, then you'll be pregnant!

ROGER: Wow . . . well, I don't know how you girls do it in Tonga, but in NZ and the rest of the world, things are a bit different. [Laughs.]

Mele imitates Rogers laugh. Lote and Peti reappear behind Roger and start pointing to him, suggesting Mele marry him. Roger turns around to see Peti and Lote.

PETI: Sooo . . . 'couple of the year'. I mean, what a year it has been. God blessing you, Mele. Coming here, all the way from Tonga, and meeting you, Roger. Everything happens for a reason.

LOTE: Yeah. Hey, Roger, if you're not doing anything this Saturday night, you should come out with us.

The girls wink at Mele. Mele is embarrassed.

PETI: We will let Mele tell you the details. [They start to walk off.] And Roger? Be there or be square.

Lote and Peti give each other a high five and exit.

ROGER (to Mele): So, Meli, can I come to this club? Is that OK with you?

MELE: Yes, of course you can come. You know the club Lepuhā?

ROGER: Lepuhu?

MELE: No, Lepuhā. You know – 'tisikou'.

ROGER: Do you know where it is?

MELE: No!

ROGER (laughs): OK, maybe if I Google it I'll find it. So, I will see you then?

MELE: Yes. I see you there . . . [starts to walk off]. Oh, and Roger . . .?

ROGER: Yes, Meli?

MELE: Be there . . . or be . . . circle.

Roger laughs. They both exit.

Scene 10: Lepuhā

At Aunty Lahi's house. Lote and Peti are waiting for Mele to arrive.

PETI: Do you think he will come out, to the club?

LOTE: This is her only chance.

Mele enters.

PETI: Fefine, tell us – did he say 'yes'?

MELE: He said . . . 'Yes!'

The girls squeal and celebrate.

LOTE: OK, OK, now that you got him to come . . . you have to now hypnotise him.

PETI: Ko e hā?

LOTE: Si`i, we have to dress her up and look sexy.

MELE: Sexy? Hauē `oua . . .

PETI: No, Mele, Lote is right. If you want your papers then you must look sexy when we go out.

MELE: But remember what Aunty Lahi say. 'No naiti-kalapu' or we go to hell.

LOTE: Si`i, this is your only chance, OK? If you win him now, then you tell him you love him and you want to spend the rest of your life with him. And he will say [imitating Roger], 'Well, I don't know what to say?' And then you say, 'Marry me' and . . . done. You win and you get married and you get your visa.

PETI: Eww Lote! You make her sound so desperate. Mele, sometimes you have to play hard to get. It might backfire on you, but no girl should ask a man to marry her. That is just wrong. This is what you do . . . When he looks at you, look away. And then look at the other guys in the club just to make him jealous. Then you 'spray [twerk] and walk away' . . . just 'spray [twerk] and walk away.' And then he will come to you and fall on to his knees and ask you to marry him and that's how I dooze it. Mmhhmm . . .

LOTE: And . . . the moral of that story, Mele, is that Peti is still single. So stick to my idea and you will be married first thing Monday morning.

PETI: Aww, whatever! Just let yourself go, Mele. Live a little. Don't worry about me, Lote or Aunty Lahi. This is about you and what you need to do to live your dreams.

Spotlight appears. Mele stares out into space with a hopeful look.

LOTE (to Mele): Are you ready?

MELE: For what?

LOTE: Umm, durr. It's Saturday night and we just got paid. It's time to go out but first we need to do something about this [pointing to Mele's clothes]. So, I got you some clothes to try out.

PETI: Well, come on girl. We don't have all day.

Mele exits and gets ready. Song: 'I'm Coming Out' by Diana Ross. Lote and Peti put their makeup on. Aunty Lahi enters with a Taufale (Tongan broom) and starts hitting the girls to finish their chores. Aunty exits. Mele enters, all glammed up, wearing hot dress, hair out and high heels.

LOTE (to Mele): Wow! Mele, you look so hot.

MELE: Yeah, can you open the window? It hot!

PETI: No, Mele, she means you look heka vela hot.

The girls laugh and hug.

Scene 11: Outside Lepuhā

The girls move upstage. They are outside Lepuhā nightclub. Upbeat 'Island music' playing in the background.

LOTE: OK, Mele, this is Lepuhā where . . . dreams . . . come . . . true!

PETI: This is the 'moment of truth', Mele. Can you walk out with a ring on that finger, or you fly home back to Tonga? No doubt, you gonna hypnotise him with your hips, but next is the way you dance. I will show you when we get inside.

LOTE: And Mele, make sure you stay where you can see us. Don't leave or go anywhere else without us, OK? You stay here, OK?

Mele, nervous, takes the smoke from Lote and inhales. Lote and Peti are shocked.

MELE (exhales): OK, let's do this.

Dance sequence. Lights go down. Song: 'I'm Alive' by Celine Dion. The girls walk slow motion upstage and when the beat comes on they begin their dance routine. A few popular songs are remixed together after 'I'm Alive' showcasing their unique dance moves. After a few songs Lote and Peti get tired and signal to Mele they will be at the bar. Roger enters from behind and the song 'Mysterious Girl' by Peter Andre plays. Mele sees Roger and they dance together awkwardly. Roger is out of rhythm and Mele tries to get close to him, without getting hit in the face. Then a slow song plays. Roger and Mele get close and slow dance, looking into each other's eyes. Roger signals to Mele to go outside with him. Mele takes a look around for Lote and Peti, who are nowhere in sight – and walks away with Roger. They both exit.

Scene 12 – Sunday morning

It's Sunday morning. Lote and Peti meet up at the carpark looking tragic with makeup smudged all over their faces and hair everywhere.

LOTE: OMG our night was heka vela.

PETI: I know, right? So good to just let loose [laughs].

LOTE: Where's Mele?

PETI: I thought she was with you.

LOTE (laughs): Good one.

PETI: Nah, really, where is she?

LOTE: She was with you last!

Lote and Peti look at each other with horror and scream. Lote slaps Peti on the face.

LOTE: Get yourself together. You look tragic right now!

Peti slaps Lote on the face.

PETI: Your face is tragic. What is the time?

LOTE: It's 10am. OMG, she's probably at church!

PETI: How do you know?

LOTE: Faith.

PETI: OK, so I guess we're going to church like this?

Lote and Peti exit.

Scene 13 – Church

Aunty Lahi enters. Lote and Peti cautiously enter – subtly looking around for Mele.

LAHI: Ko fē `a Mele?

PETI (scared): Ko Mele ē he toileti.

LAHI: Fanongo kihe Faifekau.

FAIFEKAU VOICE-OVER: Pray for forgiveness. For the Lord knows what you have done.

Lote drops to her knees and prays.

LOTE: Lord forgive . . . Peti for losing our cousin Mele.

FAIFEKAU VOICEOVER: Tell the truth and shame the devil.

LOTE: Forgive me too, Lord. She is a good girl, who loves you, and I trust that you will keep her safe until we find her. Amen.

Dance sequence. Aunty Lahi exits. Song: 'William Tell Overture: Final' by Rossini. Lote and Peti get in car seating formation and continue their search whispering and shouting 'Mele' as they pull up outside of church, home, factory – Mele is nowhere to be found. The sun starts to go down and the last place to check is the view. Lote and Peti arrive at the view. They park their car over on the side of the road and head up the hill. To their surprise they see Mele covering Roger's eyes. Peti angrily walks over to Mele while Lote pulls her back so she does not to interrupt them. Peti agrees and they fade back into darkness.

Scene 14: The view from the top

Mele has her hand covering Roger's eyes, leading him to the same view spot that Lote and Peti had taken her to before. She lets her hand go.

MELE: You like?

ROGER: Aww, wow! Of all my years living here, I have never been up Mangere Mountain and seen this beautiful view. How do you know about this place?

MELE (smiles): Mmm . . . you like me?

ROGER: Umm . . .

MELE: Yes? No? I don't know? What?

ROGER: Yes, I do like you . . . but . . .

MELE: But you love me? I love you. We get marry tomorrow afternoon?

ROGER: Whoa. Calm down – let's not get ahead of ourselves right now. Is this how you people in Tonga get married? Just like that – 'you like me, I like you, let's get married'?

MELE: Yes!

ROGER: Oh wow . . .

MELE (changing her mind): No!

Lote and Peti sneak in, comically holding tree branches as if hiding behind them while eavesdropping.

ROGER: OK, well, the way I like to do it is like this. I would like to take you on a date, to a fancy restaurant, buy you dinner and drink wine . . . so I can get to know you a bit better.

MELE: OK!

ROGER: But there is one thing. I don't know how to say this . . .

MELE: Marry me . . . I am heka vela and I am a good girl. I am a virgin too and I luff you and I want to live my life for me, but I married to you.

ROGER: Meli, Meli, Meli . . . I'm gay!

Awkward silence.

MELE: O gay? [meaning 'OK?' Mele starts to get excited.]

ROGER: No, I mean . . .

Roger whispers in Mele's ear. Mele reacts with funny facials.

MELE: Aww, so you not like me?

ROGER: Sorry, Meli, not in that way and I am very sorry if I ever gave you the wrong impression.

MELE: But you was look into my eyes . . . and you holding me . . . and you take me away from my cousins in Lepuhā. It was a sign.

Lote and Peti walk up to Roger and point for him to leave. Roger exits.

MELE (upset): This is it. This is my life. All I want was to be here, live here, work here, marry here and now I must go back to Tonga.

Lote and Peti comfort Mele.

LOTE: Well, at least you get to go back to your parents in Tonga.

MELE (fuming): No! [To Lote] This is all your fault. You da one telling me about the seven signs – that is bull sit.

PETI: OMG, did you just swear? [Laughs.]

MELE: You tell me get marry . . . and the signs of lies. He was not like me, but you make me belief he like me and then I like him. And now my heart can't breaff . . .

PETI: Well, welcome to my world, hunny. Where guys look anywhere but here. [Points to herself.] You like someone who doesn't like you back, well that's just too bad. That's life. That's reality.

LOTE: OK, back to Mele's world. She just got her heart broken, so save your world for another time.

PETI: No! She needs to learn the hard way. I am sick of trying to make everything easy and simple for virgin Mele here. Mele good, Mele church, Mele this, Mele that and yup [to Lote] I blame you too! It's your fault Mele got her heart broken.

MELE (to Lote): Pitch.

Lote is shocked.

LOTE (to Peti): What? It was all your idea, Peti. And Mele, you had to experience it one day. This will make you stronger.

MELE: Horse sit!

PETI: Yeah, that's right, Mele, horse shit.

MELE (to Peti): Fat pitch.

Peti is shocked.

LOTE: Aww, she on a roll now.

Mele ignores them and walks off onto the middle of the road near their car. Lote chases after Mele while Peti gets angry.

PETI: Yeah, you walk away, Mele. What, you scared?

LOTE: Shut up, Peti. Mele, get off the road before you get hit by a truck.

Mele falls onto her knees in the middle of the road.

MELE: No! I have no more life now, this is the end. I only dream of coming here, and now I am here I don't want to go anywhere. So, yeah, come truck. Hit me. Take me to Heaven. I want to see God . . .

Lote reaches Mele and tries to get her off the road.

LOTE: Peti, you fat shit, come and help.

Peti is offended.

PETI: Oh Hell-to-the-No! What did you call me, you skinny bitch? I'm gonna teach you a lesson.

Peti grabs Lote and they play-fight in a comedic way. Peti chases after Lote. Lote hides behind Mele. Mele is shouting to God.

MELE (crying to the Heavens): God, why have you forsaken me?!

Peti grabs Lote and Lote grabs Mele's hair and the funny catfight begins. All three are comically fighting in the middle of the road. Lights flash up in front of them but the girls are too busy fighting to notice. The sound effect of a horn from a truck plays. It takes a second for the girls to realise what the sound is. They pause and look at each other then turn to the front. It's a truck heading straight towards them. The girls scream.

Scene 15 – Welcome to Hell

Spotlight appears. Mr Bean theme song plays. The girls are stunned and apprehensive. Theme song then cuts abruptly.

VOICE-OVER (DEVIL): Welcome to Hell, bitches. Hahaha! Hahaha! Hahaha.

On the last hahaha, he chokes and coughs.

VOICE-OVER (DEVIL) (in style of customer service rep): Welcome to Hell. How can I help you?

LOTE: Ummm, I think we got hit by a truck. We were in the middle of the road and saw lights.

VOICE-OVER (DEVIL): Do you know what kind of truck? Was it a big one? Small one?

MELE: Yeah, a pig one.

PETI: Please tell me this is a dream. Please tell me we're at Spookers!

VOICE-OVER (DEVIL): Well, why were you in the middle of the road in the first place?

LOTE: She wanted to end her life so she walked onto the middle of the road thinking we would go to Heaven. But I guess not.

Mele feels bad.

PETI: She called me a fat shit and I don't appreciate a skinny 'B' like her saying that, so, yeah. I had to put her in her place.

The girls start arguing.

VOICE-OVER (DEVIL): Silence! I'm going to give you two options. Option number one: You can stay here with me and become a citizen of Hell and burn in the eternal flames forever and ever by selling your soul to the Devil to become rich and famous like Rihanna and Jay Z ... or ...

The girls think about it.

MELE: I will never sell my soul to the Devil, for I serve the one and only true Kod and that is Kod himself!

VOICE-OVER (DEVIL): Koddd? Haaaaaa! Where's your Koddd now? He could've come down from heaven and saved you, but he didn't. Aw so sad, so sad.

LOTE: Well, Rihanna is hot.

PETI: Oh shut up. I'm Rihanna and you're Jay Z.

VOICE-OVER (DEVIL): All of you, shut up. Option number two. There's this little game I like to play and if you play this game and win then you will become a citizen of Heaven. But there can only be one, now which one?

PETI: Me! I'm the one. Sorry, ladies, but every man for themselves. I'm playing the game and if you two want to play then good luck cause I'm going to win.

LOTE: It's your fault we're here.

MELE: It was all my fault. I was the one walk on the road.

PETI: Shut up, Mele, this is not about you anymore and your citizenship! This is about me going to be a citizen in Heaven.

MELE: Yeah? OK, let's see what you got.

LOTE: OK, may the best siana win.

VOICE-OVER (DEVIL): Awwww, so sweet. Not.

Song – 'O Fortuna' by Carl Orff. Girls prepare for a wrestling match. They all break out into a krump set. The song fades but Mele is still krumping, going overboard. The other two girls stare at her. She stops.

VOICE-OVER (DEVIL): All right, listen up. There are three rounds. First round is a test of the body, second round a test of the mind, and the third round a test of the spirit. First contestant to pass two out of three rounds will become a citizen of heaven. Let the games begin! Round one. The body.

The girls begin to stretch.

VOICE-OVER (DEVIL): The first contestant to give me 10 star jumps wins. Go.

The girls do star jumps. Lote is good at star jumps, Peti is slow and unfit and Mele is jumping literally trying to catch the stars.

VOICE-OVER (DEVIL): And the winner is . . . Lote.

Lote celebrates.

VOICE-OVER (DEVIL): Round two. The mind. The first person to answer this question wins. What is the highest cause of obesity amongst Pacific Islanders in New Zealand?

PETI: KFC!

VOICE-OVER (DEVIL): KFC is correct.

Peti celebrates.

VOICE-OVER (DEVIL): That's one to Lote. One to Peti. Round 3 – the spirit round. First contestant to complete this famous Bible verse wins. The Lord Is My . . .

PETI: Hope!

LOTE: Friend!

MELE: Sebberd.

VOICE-OVER (DEVIL): Sorry, Mele, what was that?

MELE: Sebberd!

VOICE-OVER (DEVIL): I couldn't quite catch that. Did you say shepherd?

MELE: Sebberd!

VOICE-OVER (DEVIL): Shepherd?

MELE: Yes. Se-bberd!

VOICE-OVER (DEVIL): Close enough. Shepherd is correct!

Mele celebrates.

VOICE-OVER (DEVIL): Since you've all won one round each, that takes us to our fourth and final round . . .

Game show build-up sound effect.

VOICE-OVER (DEVIL): The bonus round! Whichever name I pick out of this hat must answer the final question.

Devil reaches into an imaginary hat and picks out a name

VOICE-OVER (DEVIL): Oh look, Mele, it's you. Alright, Mele, let's see if you can answer this final question. If you answer this question correctly you will become a citizen of Heaven. And because you wanted to become a citizen of New Zealand . . . what is the first word of the New Zealand national anthem?

Mele has no idea. She looks to Lote and Peti but they look away, hoping she doesn't get it right.

MELE: I don't know what it is but I know I couldn't live with myself if I had to leave you two behind.

PETI: I can live with myself actually because I know the word. [Sings]: 'God of nations at thy feet.'

The Devil slowly disappears. Mele is stunned.

LOTE (to Peti): Ohh so your true colours come out now, you selfish! Shame you probably can't even fit through Heaven's gates.

Mele drops to her knees to pray.

MELE: God forgive me, I was forgetting about you. I should have tell you everything and give you everything, thanks and struggle, for I know you watch over me. I am not the best and I make mistakes but I will always come back to you and love you forever. You are God. Amen.

The girls all cry and come together, hugging each other.

LOTE: I'm sorry I called you a fat shit.

PETI: I'm sorry I called you skinny 'B'.

MELE: I'm sorry I was walk on the middle of the road.

Scene 16: Another chance

The girls hug and make up. Lights flash up (just like before). Girls look. Sound effect of horn from truck plays. Girls scream. The girls look up and brace for impact but there is no truck The girls are at home. Song – 'Hallelujah Chorus' by George F. Handel. The girls jump up with joy, hugging and high-fiving each other. Suddenly Aunty Lahi enters from the side holding a Taufale (Tongan broom).

LAHI: Shhh! Today is a Sunday. Mele, alu cook the food. Lote, wash the dishes. Peti, clean the toilet. I go rest because it's a Sabbath.

The girls look to each other and then to the audience.

GIRLS: Sai ē!

Darkness.

The End

INKY PINKY PONKY

LEKI JACKSON-BOURKE AND `AMANAKI PRESCOTT-FALETAU

Inky Pinky Ponky

Written by Leki Jackson-Bourke
and ʻAmanaki Prescott-Faletau

About the authors

Leki Jackson-Bourke is a graduate of the Pacific Institute of Performing Arts, and an emerging Pasifika artist who has toured both nationally and internationally with New Zealand theatre companies, including Massive Theatre Company, Kila Kokonut Krew and Armstrong Creative. His international tours include: Massive Company's *The Brave* (Hawaii Tour, 2015), *The Factory* by Kila Kokonut Kru (Adelaide Cabaret Festival, 2014; Edinburgh Fringe Festival, 2014), *My Name is Pilitome* by Vela Manusaute (Niue Arts Festival, 2015). Leki received the 2015 Auckland Is My Playground Award for Youth Leadership in Performing Arts awarded by Auckland Council. Aside from acting, Leki is also an aspiring writer, producer and choreographer, and recently co-produced Victor Rodger's *Club Paradiso*.

ʻAmanaki Prescott-Faletau has been dancing since the day she could walk – from contemporary to voguing, she's done it all. She is actively involved in the hip-hop dance scene, and has been a judge at the New Zealand Hip Hop Nationals. Choreography credits include: work for Lima Dance Productions and the Street Dance New Zealand National Championships (2011 Vogue Dance Crew). She has also choreographed for Auckland Theatre Company's *Checkout Chicks, The Musical* and Kila Kokonut Krew. ʻAmanaki is a key member of Fine Fatale, a transgender and gay dance company, and she was crowned Fresh Factor pageant winner in 2012. Theatre credits include *Teen Faggots Come To Life* (2014 Pride Festival) and Victor Rodger's award-winning *Girl on a Corner* (Auckland Fringe Festival). She was awarded the Best Newcomer Award at the 2014 Auckland Theatre Awards and she is a proud graduate of the Pacific Institute of Performing Arts.

Synopsis

It's ball season and hormones are on the rise at St. Valentines High. The new arrival of the fabulous fakaleiti Lisa causes a stir and she soon falls head over heels in love with First XV captain Mose. As love blooms, Lisa soon realises that behind every Prince Charming is a hater in the midst.

Acknowledgements

PIPA – The Pacific Institute of Performing Arts, Olivia Taouma and Lima Productions, Sean Coyle, Anapela Polataivao, Victor Rodger, Mario Gaoa, Letti Wickman, Lauren Jackson, Samantha Scott, Auckland Theatre Company and Lynne Cardy, Fasitua Amosa, Bob Savea, Mosese Uhila, Italia Hunt, Luse Su`a Tuipulotu, Joanna Mika-Toloa, Julianna Sopoaga, Shauntelle Jones, KC Throne Myers, Troy Tu`ua, Onetoto Ikavuka, Maxine Kalolo, Lolo Fonua, Paul Fagamalo, Nastassia Wolfgramm, Vita Vaka, Rosalind Tui, Taofia Pelesasa, Natasha Tamiano, John Afamasaga, Idaleen Williams, Lologa Lologa, Petmal Lam, Zandra Ah-Jay Maepu.

First performance

Inky Pinky Ponky received script development under the Lima Productions Writers' Workshop organised by Olivia Taouma. It premiered on July 10, 2015 at Auckland's Basement Theatre as part of Auckland Theatre Company's Next Big Thing Festival. Later in 2015 the script was also awarded the Playmarket Best Teenage Script Award under the Playmarket Plays for the Young Competition.

Cast

LISA/LEWIS: Khloe Lam-Kam
MOSE: Haanz Fa`avae-Jackson
SIA: Jahna Batts
DEMETRI: Jono Soo-Choon
LEO: Isaac Ah Kiong
BRITTNEY: Lyncia Muller
MUM: Lila Pese
MR. JENSEN: Edwin Beats
COACH: Natasha Hoyland

MRS. MANUHUHU: Talia-Rae Mavaega
PIZZA GUY: Takerei Komene

Crew
WRITERS: Leki Jackson-Bourke and ʻAmanaki Prescott-Faletau
DRAMATURGS: Mario Gaoa and Victor Rodger
DIRECTOR: Fasitua Amosa

Inky Pinky Ponky

Scene 1: The new boy

Classroom set-up. A pre-recorded track of the nursery rhyme 'Inky Pinky Ponky' plays. Second track – 'Take Me There' by Blackstreet – plays. LISA, MOSE, SIA, DEMETRI, LEO and BRITTNEY enter one by one. MR. JENSEN enters.

MR. JENSEN: Good morning, boys and girls.

EVERYONE: Good morning Mr. Jensen.

MR. JENSEN: Jensen, Jensen, that's my name. Praise the Lord. [Sings] In the name of the Father and of the Son and of the Holy Spirit.

EVERYONE (sings): Amen.

Students close eyes and assume prayer position, with the exception of Lisa. Mr. Jensen signals to Lisa to close her eyes.

MR. JENSEN (melodramatic): Dearest, dearest father in Heaven, I pray that the sun may shine bright upon these young men and women. May they realise that their bodies belong to the body of Christ. May these young males and females follow the path of Adam and Eve, not Adam and Steve. We ask this prayer through Christ our saviour.

EVERYONE (sings): Amen.

MR. JENSEN: Ahhhh, we have a new boy.

Class look around, confused. Mr. Jensen pulls out a piece of paper and reads.

MR. JENSEN: Lewis Kailu?

Class giggle at Lisa's last name as Kailu is an insult in the Tongan language.

MR. JENSEN (to class): Settle down, you trolls. [To Lisa] Lewis?

Mr. Jensen signals for Lisa to stand.

MR. JENSEN: Introduce yourself.

EVERYONE (chanting): Introduce yaself, introduce yaself.

Lisa looks lost.

MR. JENSEN: Hello . . . ?

LISA: Who me?

MR. JENSEN: Yes you! Couldn't be. Then who stole the cookie from the cookie jar? You're Lewis Kailu, aren't you?

LISA: It's Lisa Kailu, thank you, Mr . . .

MR. JENSEN: Jensen, Jensen, that's my name. Welcome to my class, Lewis . . .

LISA: Lisa!

MR. JENSEN: Lewis!

LISA: Lisa!

MR. JENSEN: Fine. If you wish to be a Lisa you can be a Lisa, just remove those hoop earrings. I rebuke them, in the name of Jesus Christ, superstar.

Lisa pulls out seat and stands up.

LISA: Why? My hoop earrings complement my boys' school uniform.

Jensen puts his hand out. Lisa takes off the earrings and hands them over.

LEWIS: Hi, I'm Lisa, not Lewis. Seventeen and Tongan, which is pretty obvious . . . unless you're deaf or blind. And it doesn't take a rocket scientist to figure out that, yes, I am a fakaleiti. 3oooooooom!

Lisa clicks fingers with attitude.

MR. JENSEN: Swearing will not be tolerated in this class.

SIA: Sir, that's not a swear word.

BRITTNEY: Fakaleiti is a Tongan word.

MR. JENSEN (confused): What's Fuck-A-Lady?

LISA: IT'S . . . FAKALEITI!

DEMETRI: The same as a fafa.

LEO: A fakaleiti is more commonly referred to as transgender. Strong like a man, but pretty like a woman.

SIA: But not as pretty as me.

BRITTNEY: Just like my uncle! His name was Uncle Andy and now he's Aunty Bubbles.

LEO: Someone who embraces identity as a female, but still has traces of a male.

DEMETRI: Yeah, a fafa, duhhh.

MOSE: It's the Tongan word for FAGGOT!

Class burst into laughter and repeat the word faggot.

MR. JENSEN: Enough. I will not have that language in my class.

DEMETRI: Faggot.

LEO: Faggot is actually a derogatory term used to describe homosexual men. Faggots and fafas are two totally different things, therefore I feel as though your insult is irrelevant.

MOSE: Faggot, faggot, faggot!

Lisa feels uncomfortable and walks out.

SIA: Awww, poor thing. He didn't last very long.

BRITTNEY: Sia, you egg. It's sheeeee, not heeee!

SIA: No, it's obviously a heeee.

MOSE: It's obviously a faggot.

Class burst into laughter again.

MR. JENSEN: Mose! That word is unacceptable. I'm sending you for after-school detention.

DEMETRI: For what, calling him a faggot?

MR. JENSEN: And detention for Demetri. Anyone else?

MOSE: That's just wrong, sir. He was born a boy. He's a homo.

MR. JENSEN: Enough! I won't hear any more of it. After-school detention this whole week.

MOSE: But we got training for 1st XV finals, sir. Coach said no one is allowed to be on after-school detention.

MR. JENSEN: Oh well, let's just all sip on a big fat cup of peace and acceptance then. I will not tolerate discrimination of any form, do you understand, Pontious Pilot? Sia, can you go and see if he's OK.

SIA: What?

MR. JENSEN: Come on, child. WWJD?

Jensen signals for Sia and Brittney to go and check up on Lisa.

Scene 2: After class gossip

Lisa is in the bathroom wiping her make-up off and looking in the mirror. Brittney and Sia approach.

SIA: Hey, you know you're not meant to be in the girls toilets, eh?

BRITTNEY: Sia!

Brittney signals to Sia to stand back.

BRITTNEY: You're the new chick, eh?

Brittney goes to high-five her.

BRITTNEY: Aw, you're so pretty.

Sia pulls Brittney back.

BRITTNEY: I'm just trying to help *her*.

SIA: *He* doesn't need your help.

BRITTNEY: *She* doesn't need your help.

SIA (same time as Brittney): Everyone needs my help, because I'm the queen. I'm all that. He's not gonna listen to you. I'm the head girl – he should listen to me.

BRITTNEY (same time as Sia): It's not about you. She needs my help because I know what she's going through and, straight up, I've been through it before.

Lisa walks out. Brittney and Sia chase after her.

BRITTNEY: Hi I'm Brittney, fefe harks?

Lisa is on edge, she doesn't know how to react.

BRITTNEY: I'm Tongan as well btw, and OMG, like, TB-Haytch, I've always wanted a fakaleiti in our class.

LISA: You're Tongan and your name's Brittney?

BRITTNEY: I knowwww oi . . . so fakama, right? I'm named after my mum's midwife. Anyways, sorry about the boys, they're losers. You can hang out with the girls, if you want.

LISA: Thanks.

SIA: I'm Sia, head girl of St.Valentine's.

Bell rings. Boys walk past, heading to the tuck shop. Girls give them the evils.

SIA: Stupid Mose.

BRITTNEY: Stupid Demetri.

SIA: Ugggh, Demetri thinks he's the man just because his parents are rich.

BRITTNEY: But his fat lips are bigger than his brain.

SIA: He's so beefyn!

BRITTNEY: Welcome to St.Valentine's. What do you think?

LISA: It's . . .

SIA: Weird?

BRITTNEY: Hory?

SIA: Poor?

BRITTNEY: Ugly?

LISA: Ummm, I was gonna say it's really BROWN.

SIA/BRITTNEY: Ohhhhhh.

SIA: Well . . . we have, like, the highest number of PI students in the country.

BRITTNEY: Oi, and the highest truancy level in the country.

SIA: And the best gospel choir and Polyfest groups in the country.

BRITTNEY: And don't forget . . . THE ST.VALENTINE'S FIRST XV!

Track – 'Sweet Love' by Chris Brown – plays softly in the background. Mose, Demetri and Leo come out in rugby gears and dance in slow motion.

BRITTNEY: Oh my gosh, the St.Valentine's First XV!

Demetri blocks the view and catches the attention of the girls. His pose kills the buzz. Music stops.

SIA: Move Demetri! Gosh, so killed it.

BRITTNEY: That was so uggggs, oi.

LISA: So . . . are there really no other fakaleitis in this school?

BRITTNEY: Nope! We use to have fafas but not fakaleitis. Not since Sionce was here.

SIA: And Troyonce.

BRITTNEY: And Italionce.

LISA: What happened to them?

SIA: Same thing that happens to every fafa here. Once the boys get to them, they start dropping out like flies. Bzzz bzzz . . .

Lisa is daydreaming and looks over at Mose who is at the tuck shop. Sia and Brittney notice her and click their fingers to get her attention.

LISA: Uuuugghhh, I HATE him.

SIA: Who? Besty? He's all goods. Did you know he's the First XV captain?

BRITTNEY: Volleyball captain.

SIA: Basketball captain.

BRITTNEY: He pretty much runs this school.

SIA: You see that chicken burger he's holding. It's the most dangerous chicken burger you'll ever come across. Tender and juicy. Dripping with mayo. That's how he sucks in his victims.

BRITTNEY: OMG gooooorl, preach it, preach it!

SIA: Don't get me wrong, I love the guy. And yeah, he may have a cute smile, perfect skin, beautiful brown eyes . . .

BRITTNEY: And that sexy, gorgeous laugh that he does.

On cue, Mose does an OTT version of his laugh.

SIA: But sorry, he's a no deal.

BRITTNEY: Yup, no deal.

SIA/BRITTNEY: NO DEAL!

SIA: Trust us. I know him inside out. We've been besties for ages and he's told me about all the chicks he's got with.

LISA: What do you mean 'got with'?

BRITTNEY: You know? Like . . .

LISA: Ewwwwah.

SIA: Oh come on, Lisa, everyone our age is doing it.

Mr. Jensen walks past the girls.

BRITTNEY: Shhhh. Change the subject.

SIA: Hi Sir.

BRITTNEY: Hi Sir.

SIA: God is good!

MR. JENSEN: Praise him!

BRITTNEY: Amen.

Mr. Jensen exits.

LISA: I think I like this school.

Girls exit.

Scene 3: Training

Boys enter, running into formation. Coach improvises different exercises for them to do.

COACH: Stop. Pathetic. Absolutely 175% pathetic. Mose?

MOSE: Yes, coach.

COACH: The fitness of this team is appalling. You boys really need to shove it in there and breach those walls if you wanna win.

MOSE: Yes, coach.

COACH: This Saturday we will remain the champions of champions. We'll mow their lawns down and hit those bad boys where it hurts. Remember boys, if the front door is blocked, then hit 'em through the back door!

Coach exits.

LEO: Coach is right, guys. Discipline is imperative. This is going to be the most important rugby game of our lives.

DEMETRI: Jaaaak, eaaaazy bro.

MOSE: Yuuuup, that's what she said too.

Mose is silent and smiling. Boys stare at Mose.

LEO: There's that cryptic smile. What's going on?

Mose repeatedly raises his eyebrows to keep them guessing.

DEMETRI: Eatass.

MOSE: Straight up. I saved all her texas.

LEO: Texas is a state in America. I think you mean texts.

DEMETRI: Text is too easy, G. Got a pic?

Demetri grabs Mose's phone. They see a photo of Sia giving Mose head.

LEO: Ouuuussssh! Is that Sia?

DEMETRI: Dry Mose.

LEO: Looks like she really is the 'HEAD GIRL'.

Mose takes his phone back, proudly.

MOSE: Two words, uce. 'Chicken . . . burgaaahh'. You want dem island girls, you aim for the stomach, not the heart.

DEMETRI: How 'bout that new fafa in our class, uce. Bro, you're the man if you tap that.

MOSE: Hell, no! Sole, I ain't gay. Gotta think about the rugby game. This is my future, you know.

LEO: We have more chance of being struck by lightning than getting picked to play for the All Blacks. Your future should be the least of your concerns.

DEMETRI: Oi, straight up – that fafa could pass as a real chick.

MOSE: You should get with her then, uce! I'm meeting this new chick from St. Mary's and she's pretty hottie. See youse tomorrow, eh fa boys.

Mose does a handshake with the other boys and exits.

DEMETRI: That guy, man.

LEO: I know, right? And Sia? She's absolutely unbelievable.

DEMETRI: Wooop dee doo . . . I can get Sia.

LEO: But Mose gets all the girls.

DEMETRI: I get girls too.

LEO: Not as much as Mose.

DEMETRI: It's not about the number, shut up.

Demetri and Leo exit.

Scene 4: Buddy up!

Morning. School bell rings. Class seated. Jensen enters.

MR. JENSEN: Have you ever felt trapped before? Trapped in a box, trapped in love, trapped like Daniel in the lions' den? Well, class, guess what today's theme is? Hmm . . . Lisa?

Leo whispers the word 'trapped' to Lisa.

LISA: Ummmm, trapped?

MOSE (mimics): Ummmm, trapped?

Lisa ignores Mose.

MR. JENSEN: Correct. The theme is trapped and you are all required to write a critical report on the movie *Shawshank Redemption* starring Morgan Freeman. Before we get started, here are your buddies for this assignment.

Mr. Jensen reads his list.

MR. JENSEN: Brittney aaaaand Leo . . .

Mixed reactions from the class.

MR. JENSEN: Sia aaaaaannnddd Demetri!

Class laugh and tease.

MR. JENSEN: Lisa and Mose!

Awkward silence from class.

MOSE: That's not fair.

MR. JENSEN: Enough! Life just isn't fair, I know I know. Now part your desks like the red sea.

Class rearrange their seats, everyone complains. Mr. Jensen does a little dance. Mose and Lisa sit in silence for a while. Jensen comes over and moves their seats closer together.

DEMETRI: Ooooouuusshhh, Mose and the faaakalaydeee!

MR. JENSEN: You have ten minutes to answer the questions.

BRITTNEY: What if we haven't seen Shawshaka Invention?

LEO: All good, I can help you.

BRITTNEY: Nah, don't oi, I'll slow you down.

LEO: It's fine.

BRITTNEY: Nah honest.

LEO: Let me see.

Brittney slowly warms to the idea of Leo as her partner. They begin to work together.

LISA (to Mose): If you want me to move, just say so.

Everyone puts their heads down to work, some pull out phones and begin texting/working. Each character is spotlit during their voice-over.

SIA (voice-over): Why is he ignoring me? I gave him what he wanted. Gosh, why isn't he texting back? We should've been partnered together. But instead I'm with this fat head. Ugggghhh PMO . . . What did I do wrong, God? I miss you, Mose . . .

DEMETRI (voice-over): I can't believe they hooked up. Straight up, I just wish she'd look at me like that. I could buy her anything she wanted. And

Mose? Bro, he's nothing without me anyways. First XV can't win a game without me. Shame, he has to sit next to that fafa . . . haaaa GAAAAY!

Sia looks up and fake smiles briefly at Demetri.

DEMETRI (voice-over): Hey, she just smiled at me . . . yeeehbooy . . . I got the swakkk . . . I got the whole baaackage . . .

LEO (voice-over): *Shawshank Redemption,* wow! And Morgan Freeman! Nominated for one Tony Award and five Academy Awards and an Oscar winner. I hope Brittney isn't freaked out by my passion for one of the greatest men who ever lived . . .

Brittney looks over at Leo. Leo looks overly keen and she quickly puts her head back down and pretends to work.

MOSE (voice-over): Finals this Saturday. I can't let anything distract me. This is the most important game of the year – scouts will be there. Imagine if I get picked up for one of those overseas clubs! One day I'd be playing for the Rugby World Cup . . . ! But first I gotta finish these damn questions . . . so hard . . .

BRITTNEY (voice-over): Boring! I hate English. Who the heck watches Shawshaka Reception, or whatever it's called. Oh my gosh, look at that fly on Mr. Jensen's banana. Awww maaaaan . . . I'm sooo hungry. I wonder if Leo has any food in his bag? Nah probably just books, he's such a nerd. Glad I'm not sitting next to Demetri tho, ew . . .

In Mr. Jensen's voice-over, he is singing the lyrics to 'Do you Want to Build a Snowman?' from Frozen.

LISA (voice-over): This is so awkward. I wonder what he's thinking. He's probably waiting for the perfect moment to embarrass me. Why did this stupid teacher put me next to him? I know exactly what these kinds of guys are like. Ew . . . who does he think he is . . . and what kind of a name is Mose anyways? Ew yuck, I can't even say it properly. Mosay? Mosi? Moose . . . moosey?

Mose pulls out his phone to check his messages. Mr. Jensen sees him.

MR. JENSEN: Mose!

LISA: Mose!

MOSE: What?

LISA: Sorry.

MR. JENSEN: Phone away now.

Silence between Lisa and Mose. Lisa is embarrassed. Mose keeps trying to sneak a peek at Lisa's answers. Lisa's looking at Mose but trying not to make it obvious. She eventually looks at him and falls into a daydream. Demetri notices.

DEMETRI (to Sia): Pssst . . .

Demetri signals for Sia to look at Mose and Lisa.

DEMETRI: Mose and the fafa make a mean couple, eh?

SIA: You're dry. Do your work.

DEMETRI: Are you coming to our game this sat? We should kick it after?

SIA: Ewwwww. No thanks. I'm coming but I ain't coming for you. Me and you will never ever be friends. Besides, everyone always comes to watch Mose, OK?

Mr. Jensen walks past. Lisa wakes up out of her daydream. After a while, Mose and Lisa finally meet eye to eye. There is an awkward pause and Mose breaks the ice.

MOSE: Umm . . . do you reckon you can help me with the first answer?

LISA: Awwwww, now you want my help?

Mose looks stuck, he keeps checking the time.

MR. JENSEN: Five minutes left!

Lisa looks at Mose struggling, she grabs his paper and helps him.

LISA: Define? Like, that means definition of. You know, like . . . define love.

MOSE: It says inmate?

LISA: Oh yeah, define inmate. Like, what is the definition of an inmate?

Silence.

LISA: It's a prisoner. That's what Morgan Freeman is in the movie, a prisoner. Trapped.

MOSE: Trapped.

Mose begins to write. School bell rings.

MOSE: Shot, thanks.

MR. JENSEN: Thank you for your co-operation, class. Boys, good luck for the finals on Saturday, may the good Lord be with you all.

DEMETRI (mocking): And also with you!

Class begin to pack up. Mr. Jensen, Leo and Demetri exit. Lisa drops a pencil and Mose picks it up. Their eyes meet. Sia and Brittney observe from a distance.

MOSE: Hey bro, thanks for helping me. See you at the finals.

LISA: Don't call me bro.

MOSE: Aaaaalrightyy then. See you at finals.

Mose exits. Brittney and Sia approach.

SIA: And whaaaat was that about?

BRITTNEY: Is he hassling you again?

LISA: Nothing, he's allgoods.

BRITTNEY: Mo`oni?

LISA: Yes, egg!

Girls exit.

Scene 5: The bet

Coach enters. Boys doing shuttles up and down.

COACH: Final training done! Remember, boys, the grass is always greener when you go in deeper. If you boys bring home the gold at tomorrow's game, then free sausages and mayonnaise on me!

MOSE: Coach I just wanna thank you on behalf of the team and we just wanna say . . . [starts singing] Ua fa`afetai, ua fa`afetai, ua malie mata e vaai, ua tasi lava oe, ua tasi lava oe, i lou nei fa`amoemoe . . .

ALL: Hippy, hippy, hooray! Hippy, hippy, hooray!

Coach exits.

LEO (mimics Mose): Mose, just wanna say on behalf of the team, the boys wanna acknowledge you as captain build-ups and we've prepared a Tongan song for you.

MOSE: Shudddup!!

Boys muck around play-fighting. Demetri changes the subject.

DEMETRI: Sole, how 'bout you and *Lisa* in English today? New besty, is it?

MOSE: Sole, taaayk id issi. She just helped me with my answers.

DEMETRI: Ooooh, it's a *she* now!

MOSE: Dry.

DEMETRI: Uce . . .

Pause.

DEMETRI: You're the skux of the school. If you can make a fafa kiss you, straight up, you're the man. SKEEEEED!

MOSE: I ain't skeed – I just don't want to . . .

LEO: Wanting to do something and being nominated to do something are two different things.

MOSE: Bro, are you deaf?

DEMETRI: A hundred bucks if you can get Lisa to kiss you!

MOSE: Not even for a million! I ain't gay.

DEMETRI: I'll lend you my car for a month.

MOSE: Nope.

LEO: Come on, Demetri, I'm sure you can do better than that.

Pause.

DEMETRI: Got it. My dad gets VIP tickets to all the All Blacks Games. Make the fafa kiss you at the ball and I'll hook you up with tickets to watch the All Blacks at this year's World Cup!

MOSE: What?

DEMETRI: You have to make him want to kiss you. At the school ball. In front of everyone. If you can do that, the tickets are yours.

LEO: Two tickets to the biggest rugby event in the world! Seeing the All Blacks, the Wallabies, the Springboks, the world's greatest rugby Gods all in one stadium. One dream, your dream. One kiss, one fafa.

DEMETRI: Leo, shut up.

MOSE: Wait, so all I gotta do is make this fafa kiss me at the ball?

DEMETRI: And the tickets are all yours.

MOSE: But I don't have to actually kiss her/him, right?

DEMETRI: That's up to you, Mose.

LEO: Imagine walking into the ball with a fakaleiti and having the entire student body stare in awkward curiosity.

DEMETRI: Nah, he's got no nuts, G, cause he thinks Lisa's hot. Skeed.

LEO: Skeed.

DEMETRI: Drops.

LEO: Drops.

DEMETRI: You caaaaan't!

LEO: You caaaan't!

MOSE: I'll do it just because I'm the man and I can. Better tell your rich dad to get my tickets ready, uce.

Boys exit.

Scene 6: Home

Evening. Home. Lisa walks in and dumps her bag. Mum is sweeping.

MUM (calling out): Lewis . . . Lewis?

Lisa ignores her.

MUM: Lewis?

Lisa ignores her again and Mum chucks the broom at her.

MUM: Oku ke telinga supo? I called out to you how many times. Now you sit there like a lazy person?

LISA: Mum, I told you, don't call me Lewis. It's Lisa.

MUM: Haaaaoue. Shaaaame. I wonder what the people at the school are gonna say about you. Ko ho`o hingoa ko Lewis not Lisa.

LISA: Mum!

MUM: Tu`u, tafi the floor make sure everything's clean. And clean your face, `ai fakalelei ho`o mata!

Lisa stands and picks up the broom. She starts sweeping and daydreaming about Mose. Mum drifts in and out of the room, also cleaning.

LISA: Mum?

MUM: Koe ha? You tired already? So lazy.

LISA (angry): `Ikai, I just wanted to ask you something. Gosh, woman!

MUM: What did you say?

LISA (sweetly): Can I ask you something, please, mother?

Mum looks at Lisa.

LISA: Can I go to the school rugby game on Saturday?

MUM: No. Sindalella clean the house.

LISA: Fakamolemole, mum. All my friends are going.

MUM: `Ikai.

LISA: Mum!

MUM: No.

LISA: Please? It's just a—

MUM: Lewis, you only started the new school and you already go haua everywhere. Why you go to the rugby game he`? The fakaleiti don't play rugby. Nofo ma`u `i `api before something happens to you. Manatu`I the three rules. School home, school home, and . . .

LISA: School home. Never mind. Forget it.

MUM: Son . . . I'm only trying to help you..

Mum tries to comfort Lisa. Mum exits.

Scene 7: The rugby game

Game day. Coach gives final prep speech.

COACH: Today's the day! Hard and fast boys – in and out, in and out. Make sure you fill those holes. It's all about pace and speed! In between every tight, wet gap you can find.

BOYS: Yes coach.

COACH: Let's walk the talk and bring those big balls to the field. You know boys, there was a great philosopher by the name of Sir Jason De Rildo and he always said: 'The biggest, fattest, juiciest mountain you climb will always have a big, long, black polar bear standing in its way.' Let's do this!

BOYS: Yeeeaaahhh!

COACH: St. Valentine's, on three: 1, 2, 3.

BOYS: ST. VALENTINE'S!

Coach and boys exit. Girls enter and take their positions as audience members. Mrs Manuhuhu enters.

MRS. MANUHUHU: Welcome to today's game, St.Valentine's vs. North Shore College for the Secondary Schools First XV title of the champions of the champions in the country. Give it up for St. Valentine's.

Boys run on field. Girls cheer.

MRS. MANUHUHU: And now, Sia Lemalu Stowers will lead the St. Valentine's school anthem.

Sia steps forward. Cast step into formation to sing school song. Sia uses this as an opportunity to show off and flirt with Mose.

EVERYONE: St. Valentine's in your mouth. We come from the dirty south. All day, every day. St.Valentine's is here to stay. St. Valentine's, St.Valentine's: realise, recognise.

Boys huddle.

MOSE (motivating): This is what it comes down to, boys. Put yourselves on the line. Mind, heart, body, soul. Everything. Let's show St. Valentine's what we got. Lehhhgooo!

Cue – horn blow. Game begins.

MRS. MANUHUHU: And they're off! A fierce start from St. Valentine's. They appear to be on the attack straight away!

Music plays – 'Bend ova, Lil' Jon'. Boys start running and passing, stylised physical theatre. Rugby in slow motion. Mr. Jensen runs past in normal time, holding a sign that says 39 minutes later. Mose drops the ball, distracted by Lisa. Whistle blows, music ends.

Crowd give a disappointed sigh. Slow motion ends. Demetri and Leo turn against Mose. Boys freeze and lights fade out on them, focus shifts to Manuhuhu who is lit up.

MRS. MANUHUHU: And it's half-time! There appears to be some tension in the St. Valentine's team. On a brighter note, the Huhu family are selling food plates on my right. If anyone would like to purchase a $5 plate of chop suey, salati paka and pani keke please go and see the big fat lady with the gifo ko'ula standing there in a bright orange puletaha.

Lights fade out on Mrs Manuhuhu, lights fade up on boys. They drop their last freeze frame and they resume scene.

DEMETRI: Bro, what's your buzz? We would've scored.

MOSE: Sorry, uce, I caked it.

DEMETRI: Learn how to catch properly, man.

LEO: Guys, calm down.

DEMETRI: You calm down, bro. We would've got that try and we would've been in the lead.

MOSE: Uce, it's not like I did it on purpose.

LEO: Look guys, I'm sure we can identify the issue, collaborate together, and—

MOSE/DEMETRI: Shut up, Leo!

Boys exit to get water.

MRS. MANUHUHU: Half-time is almost up and if St. Valentines don't pull themselves together, they risk losing their title as the champions of the champions in the country, and all their hard work will be flushed down the toileti. Yep, you heard me, down the toileti!

BRITTNEY: Sis, you made it! Ouuush, you fo'i hottie!

LISA: What's happening?

SIA: Besty just dropped the ball. Like, seriously, he never drops the ball.

BRITTNEY (to Lisa): Maybe it's cause you came looking so hot, haaaue. Distracting the players much?

SIA: No, they're just tired. Go Besty! Come on!

Boys re-enter.

MRS. MANUHUHU: Second half begins!

Cue – horn blows. Boys get back into game. Demetri scores the first try.

MRS. MANUHUHU: And Demetri Makahana appears to have scored the first try of the game.

Girls do a monotone cheer.

BRITTNEY: Oh my gosh, Demetri scored a try.

SIA: Oh my gosh, he's still a loser.

LISA: Oh my gosh, he's looking at us.

BRITTNEY: I think he's waiting for us to cheer.

SIA: So not gonna clap, oi.

LISA: Hashtag awkward.

Boys reset. Mose scores the second try.

MRS. MANUHUHU: Wow, what a try that was. Running fiercely through all the North Shore College defenders. Captain Mose is on fire!

EVERYONE (cheering): Go Mose! Go Mose! Go, go, go, Mose! [x2]

SIA: That's my besty! Shot, besty! Go besty!

Mose waves at the girls. Sia blows kisses.

MRS. MANUHUHU: And less than a minute to go, pressure is on!

Boys get back into final run. Mose scores the last try. Horn blows. Everyone cheers.

MRS. MANUHUHU: Ahhh McCain, you've done it again! St. Valentine's First XV have managed to hold on to their title as the champions of the champions in the country! My name is Mele Manuhuhu, reporting for Pepelo TV.

Mrs. Manuhuhu exits. Girls walk up to congratulate boys.

Scene 8: Plant the seed

BRITTNEY (shy): Hey Leo, I've never ever seen you play like that before.

LEO: I'm one of those conservative guys. Save it all for the field.

BRITTNEY: Ooooh, I love those kind of guys.

DEMETRI: What about me? Did you see my cool try?

SIA: No one cares. Mose was the man of the match.

MOSE: YUUUUUUUSSS!!! WE WON!!!

Everybody cheers, Mose notices Lisa. Pause.

MOSE (to Lisa): Oh 'Sup.

DEMETRI (teasing): Hi Lisa.

Lisa smiles.

MOSE: Honest to who, you came! The man. Thought you'd be too cool. Then I saw you dancing and cheering, pretty loud outside of school, eh.

SIA (singing/attention-seeking): I can be loud too. I mean, I can sing loud. Did you hear me sing the school song? Ouuusssh! I know, right?

BRITTNEY: Sis, hitting dem Mariah Carey notes

SIA (serious): Brittney, don't kill the buzz.

BRITTNEY: Ooops, I did it again!

LEO: You can totally kill my buzz if you want. How 'bout a milkshake?

BRITTNEY: Yum! Keeen.

Brittney starts to sing lines from 'Milkshake' by Kelis. Leo and Brittney exit.

DEMETRI: So, what are you up to now, Sia? I'll shout us a feed.

SIA: Shhh, not now. Besty, what do you have planned?

MOSE: Probably just home. What about you, Lisa?

LISA: Yeah, just home as well.

DEMETRI: Where do you stay? Maybe Mose can walk you home, eh, Mose?

Demetri nudges Mose, Mose fake smiles.

LISA: No, it's too far. I live near Mt. Roskill.

DEMETRI (excited): Honest to who, don't you stay near Mt. Roskill, Mose? Aw, there's no way!

SIA (angry): No fricken way!

Everyone looks at Sia.

SIA (happy): I meaaaan . . . yaaaay!

DEMETRI: Yay, Mose's gonna walk you home. Right, Mose?

Lisa is silent.

MOSE: It's all good, I'm going that way.

LISA: I'm alright, honest.

MOSE: Are you too cool to walk with me?

SIA: I'll walk with you, Mose.

MOSE: You live in Otara.

Mose turns to Lisa.

MOSE: Come on, let's go.

SIA (interrupts): Besty, come!

Sia grabs Mose and walks him to the side.

SIA: Like, what the hell, man? Why are you avoiding me?

MOSE: I'm not. I just been busy.

SIA: Then how come you didn't reply to my Facebook mail? You're such an eatass, Mose, don't even try and lie. It said SEEN on the mail, and the little green dot thing said you were online. You so PMO. Ygggh.

Lisa sees them talking and goes to leave. Mose notices and tries to follow her.

MOSE: I gotta go.

Mose kisses Sia on the cheek and exits.

SIA: Oh, hell no! You're ditching me to hang with Lisa? Check yourself, Mose. Like wat da eff?

Pause.

SIA (sighs)

DEMETRI: Looks like it's just the two of us.

SIA: Don't even try it.

DEMETRI: Try what?

SIA: Get lost.

DEMETRI: Bro, what's your problem?

SIA: I don't have a problem, and I'm not your bro!

DEMETRI: Calm lalo.

SIA (angry): Ew, shut up! Don't act like you know me. You don't even understand anything – you're just a stupid boy and all boys are stupid! Uuuuuggghhh... You don't even understand.

DEMETRI: Understand what?

SIA: Nothing.

Silence.

DEMETRI: I see the way you look at Mose. I've seen all the girls look at Mose the way you look at him. It's all good.

Sia gives up. Demetri is the only person left to talk to. She slowly gives in.

SIA: It's just... well, how would you feel if someone you liked just walked past you daily and acted like you didn't exist? How would you feel knowing that you go through all this extra trouble to stand out, but the one person you want attention from won't even look at you? How would you feel if you spoke so loud but the one person you wanted to hear, just wouldn't listen to a single word? I'm just... I dunno... I'm tired of trying... I'm actually tired of trying!

DEMETRI: Me too. Wanna pash?

SIA: Ew! Tooo far, dickface.

DEMETRI: Jokes, jokes. Wait... I can help you get what you want.

Sia stares at Demetri in silence.

DEMETRI: I can help you get Mose.

SIA: Whatever.

Sia goes to leave.

DEMETRI: Nah, honest. Come to the ball with me and I promise you Mose will be yours by the end of the night.

SIA: Whaaaat the hell? You're dreaming! I'm so not going to the ball with you. Creeep! Iaaa faa faa yerrr faa. CREEEEP!

Sia starts to leave again.

DEMETRI: I already know you got with Mose – he told me everything.

Pause.

DEMETRI: He bought you a chicken burger, right?

SIA (panicking): Oh my gosh, oh my gosh, please don't tell anyone. Even Brittney doesn't know. Oh my gosh . . .

Pause.

DEMETRI (pleading): Mose's not gonna want you if you're desperate, aaaand he already tapped you so you know he's gonna gap you. You have to play hard to get. The ball is the perfect place to do it. Come with me? It sounds dumb but straight up I know Mose – he's jealous of me. And if he sees us together, he'll want you.

Pause.

DEMETRI: Sooo . . . ?

Pause.

SIA: Wait . . .

Pause.

SIA: I don't know . . .

DEMETRI: I got something else you might wanna know too, but you can't tell anyone.

Cue track – 'Creep' by TLC. Demetri and Sia exit.

Scene 9: Walk me home

Mose and Lisa enter. Mose is walking behind her. 'Creep' track ends.

LISA: I'll be sweet, you can go.

MOSE: What, am I that ugly that I can't even walk with you?

LISA: Dry.

MOSE: You're dry. Slow down.

Lisa continues to walk.

MOSE: So, what'd you think of the game? Pretty cool, eh? Was that your first rugby game?

LISA: No. Just cause I'm . . . the way I am . . . doesn't mean I've never been to a rugby game before.

MOSE: Oh no, no, I didn't mean it like that.

Pause.

MOSE: So where do you stay?

LISA: I'll be all good from here. Bye.

MOSE: Lisa, wait.

Mose darts out in front of her.

LISA: What do you want from me?

Mose pauses.

LISA: Come on 'Mose', don't act dumb. You know that guys like you don't hang around people like me, so what do you want?

MOSE: Nothing, I'm just—

LISA: Here to mimic the way I speak? Call me a faggot again? How original. Why don't you try: 'Lisa's a slut.' 'Lisa has Aids.' 'Lisa gives the best head in the school.' 'Cos that's what my last school used to say. Better work stories, Mose. Bye.

MOSE: I'm sorry, I had no idea.

LISA: Well, now you do.

MOSE: Straight up I just . . . I been a dick . . .

LISA: Yup.

MOSE: I honestly feel stink, eh . . .

LISA: Care.

MOSE: You came to support my game. I owe you.

LISA: Yes, you do owe me, but I didn't come to support you.

MOSE: And I'm sorry for calling you a . . . faggot.

Lisa gives him the stare.

MOSE: That's just my . . . sense of humour.

LISA: Ha ha, you're sooooo funny! Jump off a bridge and die.

MOSE (gasps): That's how my first brother died.

Pause.

MOSE: Jokes.

They stare at each other. She realises Mose's laughing and they both laugh. Mose puts his hand out to introduce himself properly.

MOSE: Mose.

Lisa sees some remorse in Mose's eyes. She looks at his hand and Mose does not move. She opens her bag and pulls out hand sanitiser. She drops some sanitiser on Mose's hand and signals him to clean his hands. He does. Then she shakes his hand.

LISA: Lisa.

Scene 10: Mum at home

Lisa sneaks in. Mum hides in silhouette.

MUM: Hello, Lewis. How was your day?

LISA: Mum.

MUM: Ha`u.

LISA: I was just . . .

MUM: Koe fiha eni?

LISA: Mum, I'm sorry I . . .

MUM: Koe ha `uhinga oku ke ta`e fanongo mai ai? Ta`e `ofa, you ungrateful.

LISA: I'm not ungrateful.

MUM: He vave `a e ngutu ke ansa back at me. Tapuni.

LISA: It's just a rugby game, gosh.

MUM: No. I don't care about da rugby game. Kou tala atu keke nofoma`u `i `api. I saw you walking home with a boy. What if the people see? The people will talk Lewis, they will always talk!

LISA: Mum, will you just listen to me please?

MUM: You think you're grown up now? Why do you think your dad left?

Pause.

MUM: He left because he didn't know how to look after you! I'm the only one who loves you.

LISA (mumbles): God loves me.

MUM: Koe ha?

Pause. Lisa sits quietly. Mum snaps.

MUM: Ha'u ki heni.

Pause.

MUM: Come here now!

Mum aggressively wipes Lisa's face to try and remove the make-up. Lisa struggles to hide her face but does not fight Mum back.

MUM: I'm doing this for your own good, Lewis. One day you will thank me.

Scene 11: Waggers

Bell rings. Period 6. Brittney and Lisa crawl on stage, hiding from teachers.

LISA: Oi, if we get snapped I'll get in so much trouble.

BRITTNEY: We won't! I've wagged here since third form. Trust me, I'm from Ma`ufanga, OK?

LISA: Pssssht Lapaha all day . . .

BRITTNEY: Awww, what a shame. Maybe next time.

Brittney pulls out phone.

BRITTNEY: Oi sis, but TB-Haytch, I had to show you this. It was all over Facebook this morning.

Lisa looks confused. Brittney shows her screen.

LISA: What the hell? OMG – who took that?

BRITTNEY: Everyone's been talking about it. Ousssh, I can't believe Mose walked you home. Do you know how big that is?

LISA: Ew, who uploaded the photo? I don't even remember taking a photo with him!

BRITTNEY: It's on Demetri's page, it's so weird. I'd be careful, sis. Looks like those Snapchat ones.

LISA: OMG, ew. Arrrghhh, I look so fat! I look like Precious.

Brittney shows Lisa the phone again. Lisa reads.

BRITTNEY: Read the comments, sis. Mose's comment.

LISA: I don't wanna know, it's probably something bad. I knew it was a trick – they just wanted to mock me!

BRITTNEY: Awwww pity partyyyyy! Read!

Lisa reads Mose's comment, then she smiles.

BRITTNEY: If you knew Mose like I do, you'd know he doesn't stick up for many chicks. TB-Haytch, sis, you're so fo'i toxic right now, everyone's commenting about you, saying she's so lucky, she's a star, oouuuuaaa!

Brittney teases, Lisa goes quiet.

BRITTNEY: Lisa, what's wrong? Did I say something?

LISA: Nah, just thinking about my old school.

BRITTNEY: What about your old school?

Pause.

LISA: I've never had this kind of attention before. At my old school . . .

BRITTNEY: I'm sure you were all that, no need to rub it in.

LISA: No, I wasn't. Shut up.

BRITTNEY: Koe ha?

LISA: Promise you won't laugh?

Brittney does the sign of the cross and then puts both palms up.

LISA: I just wanted to finish school, make my parents proud, feel accepted. The boys started a rumour that I gave them the best head . . . and that I was the tranny slut of the school. It was all over Facebook.

BRITTNEY: Awwwww . . . what's wrong with that?

LISA: Ew, you palaku! It's not true. I've never . . . you know?

BRITTNEY: Haaaaue Maaalie, Virgin Mary!

LISA: That's right!

BRITTNEY: Ohhhhhhhhh! Sis TB-Haytch, do you know what I do when I have haters?

LISA: What?

BRITTNEY: Selfies!

Brittney pulls out her phone.

BRITTNEY: Selfie ki ai!

LISA: All dat ki ai!

BRITTNEY: Wagging ki ai!

LISA: Pretty ki ai!

BRITTNEY: Beyonce ki ai!

Lisa and Brittney crack up. Leo enters unannounced. They get a fright.

LEO: It's only me. Move down, I wanna wag too!

Leo joins in.

BRITTNEY: Why aren't you in class?

LEO: Initially I was heading towards the sick bay . . .

BRITTNEY: Ew, you're not even sick, you liar.

LEO: I am definitely sick.

Leo coughs, girls stare at him.

LEO: Nah, I just finished the assignment early, then I got bored watching Demetri trying to be a creep to Sia. Those two, man, they should just go out.

BRITTNEY: I know . . . I hate it when two people like each other but they do nothing about it, eh.

LEO: Don't 'chu reckon?

BRITTNEY: I so reckon.

LEO: People just need to learn how to communicate their inner feelings for each other.

BRITTNEY: Hardout. Instead of waiting for fairy tales to come true.

Britney smiles at Lisa. Lisa brushes it off and changes the subject.

LISA: Who else was in class?

LEO: Everyone . . . umm Sia . . . Demetri . . . Mose.

BRITTNEY: Ooooh, Mose!

LISA: Ta'e. I'm gonna rip your fringe off, OK? Shut up!

LEO: Don't tell me you like Mose too? Mose's a great guy. I mean, he's absolutely awesome, right? He's an exceptionally good rugby player . . . I mean, he is a splendid character . . . He's one of a kind. I like Mose, Mose's cool.

BRITTNEY: Leo, why are you acting all weird?

LEO: I'm not. I'm just telling Lisa how great Mose is.

BRITTNEY: You know something, eh? Hurry up and spit it out.

LEO: No, no, I don't know anything. Well . . . just that Mose is a player . . . and, and Sia's obviously in love with him but won't admit it . . . but yeah, sorry Lisa, I don't think Mose's gay.

BRITTNEY: Leo, OMG awks. Shut up.

LEO: Oh weh, sorry.

Lisa feels uncomfortable and gets up to leave.

LISA: Sis, I'm just going bathroom. I'll meet you at the bus stop after school? Period's almost over anyways.

Lisa exits.

BRITTNEY: Lisa, tali. Good one, Leo.

LEO: How was I supposed to know? I'm smart but I'm not that smart.

BRITTNEY: It's not fair, I just wish everyone could get the happy ending they deserve, you know?

Leo leans in to kiss Brittney, lights fade on scene before they kiss.

Scene 12: Mose finds Lisa

Bell rings – after school.

MOSE (to Lisa): Hey, you weren't in class last period. Did you see our Facebook photo? I look pretty hot, eh.

Mose strikes a pose.

MOSE: What's wrong?

LISA: Felt sick.

MOSE: What kind of sick? Headache? Stomach?

LISA: Ummm, yeah.

MOSE: Which one. Sore head or sore stomach?

LISA: Ummm, it's hard to explain.

Lisa tries to leave.

MOSE: What's so hard? You just say: I have a sore stomach, Mose, I need to go, or; I have a headache, Mose, I need to go.

Lisa shoves Mose out of the way just as Demetri and Sia enter.

LISA: Move, egg!

SIA: Ooooh, what's going on here? Batting for the other team, eh besty?

MOSE: What do you want?

SIA: Didn't see you in English, Lisa.

MOSE: She felt sick, what's it to you?

SIA: What, are you pregnant or something? [Laughs.]

LISA: No, we all know that's impossible, but ummm . . . you look a bit pregnant, on your front, side and back.

MOSE/DEMETRI: Oooooooohhhhh!!

LISA: Jokes.

SIA: All goods, sis. I know I look hot in my *skirt*. Come on Demetri, we got research to do for our assignment. Bye besty!

Sia and Demetri exit. Lisa tries to sidestep Mose. He plays around and blocks her way.

MOSE: Oi, you hungry? Should we go get a feed?

LISA: Nah, I'm OK.

MOSE: Come on, what's your favourite food? You like ice cream?

LISA: Hmmm, nah. I'm more of a pizza kind of gal.

MOSE: Oh . . . pizza . . . uhhhh, are you shouting? I was thinking something like corned beef, taro and noodles?

LISA: Ew, that's so Southside.

MOSE: Ew, it's better than pizza.

LISA: Have you seen 'Selena'? It's my fave movie and her fave food is pizza.

MOSE (sings): A biddy biddy bumbah, ooh a biddy biddy bumbah.

LISA: Mose, move. I might miss my bus.

MOSE: Nope, I'm walking you home.

LISA: No, you're not.

MOSE: Yes, I am.

LISA: Mose!

MOSE: Lewis! I mean Lisa. Shit, sorry . . .

Lisa laughs, she slowly walks and Mose follows.

Scene 13: Baby boy

Mose and Lisa walk home. Cue song – 'Baby boy' by Big Brovaz. This scene is done like a fantasy where Mose and Lisa are living in a perfect world. Time fast forwards and we see a montage of different moments highlighting how perfect their love is. The other characters float in and out like a chorus in a fairy tale. Scene ends. Mum arrives at school to wait for Lisa. Jensen enters.

MR. JENSEN: Are you alright there?

MUM: No. I'm looking for my . . . my son Lewis. Please, I'm so worried. I was meant to pick him up after school. He was meant to wait, I told him—

MR. JENSEN (cuts mum off): Lewis who?

MUM: Kailu.

MR. JENSEN: Oooooh, Lord have mercy, you mean Lisa?

MUM: Io yes, yes . . . Do you know him?

MR. JENSEN: Yes, I'm Lisa's English teacher. Perhaps your husband picked her up?

MUM: No, no. My husband and Lewis, they not get along. He left us a long time ago. Please, I'm just so worried. They bullied him in the last school, maybe something bad happen. Lewis has been acting very different lately.

MR. JENSEN: What do you mean different?

MUM: He's been answer me back, come home late, lying to me.

MR. JENSEN: Look, Mrs. Kailu, I'm not sure if you're aware of this but at school Lewis likes to be referred to as Lisa.

MUM: 'Ikai, no, no, no! Lewis is a boy, this is a Catholic school, they should teach the kids it's wrong. You should know better! God made Lewis and God made him as a boy.

MR. JENSEN: God also made you to be . . . a parent.

Pause.

MR. JENSEN: I know this may be hard for you to understand right now, and I'm not trying to tell you how to be a good parent but . . . from my own experience, Mrs. Kailu, it's better to let your child live freely and happily than to risk losing them forever.

Mum and Jensen exit.

Scene 14: Lisa likes cheese

Home. Night time. Lisa sitting on the front doorstep.

LISA (monologue): I'm so lost right now. What if things start to get serious? I catch myself doing things I wouldn't usually do. Stealing the car to pick him up, stealing money to top him up. He's been hinting heaps about the ball. I've always dreamed of the perfect prince sweeping me off my feet. Wearing one of those beautiful peach cocktail dresses like in the movies, but what would Mum say? Mum would never let me go. This is the first school where I have felt respected and accepted, and it's all because of the power this one guy has. Has he forgotten that underneath it all I'm still a boy, or does that not even matter to him anymore? We talk for hours on the phone, sometimes until we both fall asleep. Surely that means something? He's so good to me and kind, he cares about me (sigh). I don't know. God, just give me a sign!

A pizza man arrives with a pizza box.

PIZZA MAN: Excuse me, are you Mr. Kailu?

LISA: No, I'm Princess Kailu. Who's asking?

PIZZA MAN: I believe this is for you.

LISA: Oh, hell no, I didn't order any pizza. I ain't paying for this.

PIZZA MAN: It's already been paid for.

LISA: Is this a prank? I didn't order any pizza . . .

PIZZA MAN: No prank. There's a name left on the order.

Pizza man shows her the box. Lisa reads.

LISA: From Mose.

Pizza man hands over the box.

PIZZA MAN: Enjoy your pizza, sir. Madam!

Pizza man exits. Lisa opens the box and begins reading.

LISA: Will you be my ball partner please, or is this too cheesy? Mose xoxo

Lisa smiles and is excited. Mum arrives home. Lisa notices and drops the pizza box.

MUM: Lisa?

LISA (pleading): Mum, I'm so sorry I forgot to wait for you. Please don't be mad, Mum. I came home and you were gone and I just remembered that you were picking me up today.

MUM: Look at you! Didn't even give me the chance to speak.

LISA: I know Mum, I'm sorry, I just don't wanna fight anymore.

Pause.

LISA: Wait, did you just call me . . .

MUM: Lisa, you know . . . I struggle as a mother. I work hard to make sure you have the best . . .

LISA: Mum!

MUM: When you were born into this world, I knew something about this baby was going to be hard for me and for your dad. You always liked to play in Mum's bag and you loved the smell of Victoria Secret perfume. I knew something was wrong with this child.

LISA: Mum, kataki . . .

MUM: I love you, son. I don't have anybody left in this world to care for me when I am old. Your dad loved me and he left, and I know you are growing up and soon you are going to leave me too. Wherever you go, don't forget your home and me. I'm sorry I was so rough on you. I only want to watch out for you because I worry the world is not ready for you. But you shouldn't be afraid anymore. You go out and be who you want to be. As long as you remember, Koe Otua mo Tonga ko hoku tofi`a. Nothing can stop you if you remember the Lord. As long as you know I love you and you're happy. It's not easy for me, but I will try. Ofa atu, Lisa.

Lisa hugs her mum, with a full-on, loving, don't-let-go kind of hug. Mum notices the pizza box.

MUM: Oh, did you bring pizza home! Good, I'm hungry, let's eat the pizza.

Mum reads the box.

LISA: Mum ouuuuuaaaa . . .

MUM: What colour is his tie for the ball?

LISA: What? Why?

MUM: Because we need to find a matching dress, of course.

Lisa hugs Mum.

Scene 15: Chicken burger

Bell rings – lunchtime at school. Brittney and Sia hanging out, Mose watching Leo and Demetri on chewing gum duty. Mr. Jensen floating about on duty. Lisa enters. Mose sees her and walks over to join her.

LISA: Hi. How was class?

MOSE: All good. Eh, what about you?

LISA (teasing): Same old, boring! Where's my lunch, you build-ups? Your shout, isn't it?

MOSE: Oh yeah, what do you want?

LISA: Ummmm, surprise me?

MOSE: Sweet.

Mose goes to buy Lisa lunch from the tuck shop. Brittney and Sia start gossiping about them.

BRITTNEY: Oi honest to who, sis, check that out. Mose's buying her lunch! OMG, OMG!

SIA (jealous): You mean *him* lunch. You know Lisa's a boy, right? Uuuuuggghhh.

LEO: Dox, check that out. Mose's been pretty consistent with pursuing that fafa, don't you reckon?

DEMETRI: Cause Mose's a gaybo, G.

LEO: Well, I hope you got his tickets ready.

DEMETRI: Nah, he won't bring that fag to the ball. He's drop nuts.

LISA: Everyone's looking at us. Do people know? I haven't told anyone I said yes. Did you?

MOSE: Who cares? Here, eat.

Mose hands Lisa some lunch.

LISA (serious): A chicken burger?

MOSE: Whaaaaat?

LISA: Nothing. You're fired. [Giggles.]

MOSE: I'm gonna go pay for our tickets at the office. Meet up after?

LISA: OK.

SIA (shocked): Is that . . . a chicken burger!?

BRITTNEY: In theaaaa. Oh my gosh, a chicken burger! I guess you know what that means.

SIA: It means they're hungry and they wanna eat lunch.

BRITTNEY: TB-Haytch I reckon it's something more.

Mose exits and Lisa walks over to Brittney and Sia.

LISA: Are youse hungry? Do youse want some?

SIA: 'Youse' is not a word. And no thanks, tuck shop food is straight up disgusting.

LISA: It's just a chicken burger.

BRITTNEY (joking): I knew it! You little hoe, I saw you with Mose. OMG details, details . . .

LISA: What?

BRITTNEY: Youse go out, eh?! Hurry up.

LISA: No. We're just mates.

Silence.

LISA: And he sorta asked me to the ball. Just as friends!

Lisa and Brittney scream. Sia looks over at Demetri and they smile at each other for a while.

SIA (fake): Congratulations, sis, you're gonna look so hot together. I can just see it now. You could even win King and King. You're gonna love it. I soooo wanna tell you girls who my ball partner is, but I think I'll leave it a surprise.

BRITTNEY: I can't believe it. Well, I might as well tell you all, Leo asked me to the ball too!

Girls jump up and down screaming. Mr Jensen walks over. Leo and Demetri exit.

MR. JENSEN: What is all this screaming about, girls? I hope we're screaming for the Lord! Yes, Jesus!

Mr. Jensen joins the girls and jumps up and down.

BRITTNEY: We all have ball partners, sir.

MR. JENSEN: Is that all? Oh, you teenagers. Well my advice to you all is to make sure you have fun. This will be one night you remember for the rest of your lives.

BRITTNEY: Sir, can I pay for my ticket now?

MR. JENSEN: Sure. Come on and follow me to the light, my child.

Brittney and Mr. Jensen exit.

LISA: Sooo . . . are you excited about the ball?

SIA: Just cause Mose's taking you to the ball, don't think you're bad, OK?

LISA: Look, Sia, I'm not the one chasing him. Have him.

SIA: Let's stop pretending like we like each other, eh?

LISA: Yes, let's.

SIA: You think you're the shit, but you ain't. First you steal Brittney away and get her to feel sorry for you and your little fakeass stories.

LISA: What's your problem?

SIA: You're my problem!

LISA: You know Sia, you'd actually be a pretty cool chick if you didn't try so hard.

SIA: You know, Lisa, you'd actually be a pretty cool chick if you actually were a chick. Oh, that's right . . . you're just a boy in a dress.

Lisa is stunned. Sia sees people coming so she goes to hug Lisa.

SIA (sarcastically): Enjoy it while it lasts. Lisa.

Girls exit.

Scene 16: The plan

Night time. The bus depot. Demetri enters on phone.

DEMETRI (whispers): Yo . . .? Where you at . . .?

Sia enters on the phone.

SIA: At the depot, egg. Where are you? Hurry up!

DEMETRI: Where? I'm at the depot.

Demetri spots Sia.

DEMETRI (yells): Pssst . . . Shhhhhht! Pssssst!

SIA: There's a creepy guy yelling at me! Hurry up, dick!

DEMETRI: It's me!

Demetri waves his phone light at Sia. She waves her phone back and walks over.

SIA: So . . . I've made up my mind, I'm coming with you.

DEMETRI: Yup, already knew you would.

SIA: Uggghhh. And Lisa is going with him, it's confirmed. She told the girls this morning!

DEMETRI: So he's actually taking her?

SIA: Yes.

DEMETRI: Good.

SIA: That's not good! Stupid fafa, she's so fricken confident, PMO. What do we do now?

DEMETRI: We wait. Don't worry, everything's sussed. I've paid for everything. Once he sees me with you, he's gonna wish you were his and not mine.

SIA: Ew, I'm not yours, we're only pretending, remember?

DEMETRI: Pretending, that's right.

Pause. Demetri leans in to kiss Sia.

SIA: No, no, no. OMG no.

DEMETRI: Sorry, I was getting into character, pretending!

SIA: I gotta go. Seriously, my dad's gonna kill me and then no ball. Your plan better work. Ugggh, I can't wait to see Lisa fall flat on his man face.

DEMETRI: You're pretty hot when you're angry, you know.

Sia leans in and kisses Demetri on the cheek.

SIA: Whatever . . . Bye, FRIEND!

Sia exits and Demetri watches her walk off.

Scene 17: How does it feel?

Lights up on Mose in his room. Cue track – 'How Does it Feel' by D'Angelo. Mose is trying on his ball outfit and looking at himself. He attempts to put on his tie and fails. He tries again and again. Something is bothering him. He stops and stares at himself in the mirror and begins his monologue.

MOSE: What the hell's going on with me? How did I let it get this far? I'm meant to be in control. There's just something about her. Kick back. No drama. We talk and hang like she's one of the boys. With her I can just be myself, Mose. Why aren't all girls like her? She brings out the best side of me, she's funny, thick-skinned, knows who she is and knows what she wants. She looks after me, she makes sure I have lunch, my uniform's straight, my homework's done. How do you fight a feeling that feels so right. Am I really doing this?

Scene 18: The ball

Cue Song – 'My My My' by Johnny Gill. Disco light comes on. Mr. Jensen dances his way in. He is there early prepping everything. He stands ready to greet everyone with Holy Water. Brittney and Leo enter.

MR. JENSEN: Welcome to the ball. When Jesus says yes, nobody can say no. Halleluija. Bless you.

LEO: Thank you, sir.

BRITTNEY: He's so weird.

LEO: Just smile.

Sia and Demetri enter together.

MR. JENSEN: Welcome, Samson and Delilah.

Demetri and Sia smile at Mr. Jensen. They walk over to Brittney and Leo and greet them.

BRITTNEY: Girl, you looook so hotttt! Capital Haytch hot!

SIA: Tonight's the night.

LEO: Baby we're just gonna grab some cold beverages. Do you want anything?

BRITTNEY: I'm all good. Thanks baby.

Leo and Demetri walk away.

SIA: Baby even?

BRITTNEY: I know, right? Hit me baby, one more time!

Sia and Brittney chat amongst themselves.

LEO: Skux bro. You and Sia?

DEMETRI: Told you bro, she's easy. She liked me from the start.

LEO: So what, are you guys an official item now?

DEMETRI: Yeahboooy.

Demetri and Leo look over at the girls.

BRITTNEY: That's so cool you decided to come with Demetri.

SIA: Oi, I told you, I felt sorry for him. Friendzone!

BRITTNEY: Don't be sad, you guys are cute.

SIA: Dry. I sooo better win Queen for this. Vote for me.

BRITTNEY: Hafff tooo. Just vote me and Leo for cutest couple.

MR. JENSEN: Aw, you girls look beautiful. Remember Mary, mother of Jesus, not Mary Magdalene tonight, k girls? Sia, that dress is amazing. My wife used to have one just like that.

Mr. Jensen walks over to the boys.

SIA: Ewwwww, I so wanna change my dress now.

BRITTNEY: Oh my gosssh . . . is thaaaat . . .?

Cue song – 'Spend my Life' by Eric Bennet and Tamia. Mose and Lisa enter, heads turn to stare at them. Brittney approaches. Sia eyes them out.

MR. JENSEN (on the microphone): Ladies and Gents, welcome to the ball of all balls. The St. Valentines <current year> school ball. Hosanna, bless the Lord. Remember students, your body is a temple of the Holy Spirit. Just saying. Gentlemen, take your partners to the dance floor.

Music resumes at low volume. Mr. Jensen exits. Sia and Demetri move to the front and dance in the spotlight. Everyone else freezes. Sia sneaks an alcohol shot before anyone sees.

SIA: Why isn't he looking at me?

DEMETRI: I'm looking at you.

SIA: Yeah, but Mose's not!

DEMETRI: Be patient.

SIA: We don't have all night.

DEMETRI: You gotta make him jealous. Here.

Demetri grabs Sia and they dance close together.

SIA: Better?

DEMETRI: Hell yeah.

Demetri and Sia dance their way to the back. Brittney and Leo dance their way to the front.

BRITTNEY: Hun, have you voted yet?

LEO: Not yet, but I might just vote for Lisa and Mose as King and Queen.

BRITTNEY (angrily): Why aren't you voting for me?

LEO: Because you don't need Queen to prove anything. You're already my queen.

BRITTNEY: Awwww . . . cheeesy. But cute.

Brittney and Leo dance their way to the back. Mose and Lisa dance to the front.

MOSE: Are you having fun?

LISA: Are you?

MOSE: I asked you first.

LISA: So, I asked you second. What's your point?

MOSE: You're an egg.

LISA: You're a bacon.

Mose and Lisa dance their way to the back. Sia and Demetri dance to the front.

SIA: Seriously, your plan's not working.

DEMETRI: Be patient.

SIA: I'm sick of waiting.

DEMETRI: Yeah, aren't we all.

Demetri and Sia dance their way to the back angrily. Demetri accidentally steps on Sia's toe. Brittney and Leo dance their way back to the front.

BRITTNEY: Something's up.

LEO: Like what?

BRITTNEY: I don't know, I just got weird feelings. Tell me I'm crazy.

LEO: You're crazy.

BRITTNEY: Yeah, I think I am.

LEO: I like crazy.

Brittney and Leo dance their way to the back and Mose and Lisa dance their way to the front.

LISA: What is it?

MOSE: It's just . . . nothing.

LISA: What, egg?

MOSE: You.

> *Pause.*

MOSE: You're different.

> *Pause.*

MOSE: I've been with heaps of chicks and, like, it's just . . . I mean there's no such thing as the perfect chick.

> *Pause.*

MOSE: But I think I'm . . .

> *Pause.*

MOSE: I mean I think I . . .

LISA: Shhhh . . .

MOSE (looks down): Sorry.

LISA: Don't be.

> *Pause. Lisa pulls Mose's head up.*

LISA: You're such a nice guy, Mose. I feel like a princess every time I'm with you.

Pause.

LISA: I don't know . . . I don't want you to . . .

Pause.

LISA: Well, things would be different if I was a real . . . you know . . .

MOSE: But that's just it. I don't care what they say. But before anything happens, Lisa, I want you to know I caught feelings I never meant to catch. I can honestly say I've fallen in love with you for who you are, and not what you look like.

Silence. Lisa closes her eyes and leans in for the kiss. However, the kiss is interrupted by Sia who grabs the microphone.

SIA: Aaaaaaand CUT!

Lights snap on.

SIA: Congratulations everyone, the votes are in! And Mose, you have won.

Demetri tries to grab the microphone off Sia.

DEMETRI: Sia, not like this.

SIA: Everybody, it's time the truth came out! Mose, would you like to come up and say your victory speech?

LISA: What is she talking about?

MOSE: Nothing. Let's go.

Mose tries to grab Lisa but she stays to listen.

SIA: Come on, Mose, the stage is all yours!

DEMETRI: Sia that's enough!

BRITTNEY: What's going on?

SIA (to Lisa): Mose got dared by the boys to make you kiss him at the ball.

Mose runs to collar Demetri.

SIA: And it looks like it worked. Shot, Mose!

Mose holds Demetri by his collar. Lisa turns and looks at Mose.

SIA: We all know Mose wouldn't really fall for this freak. Cheers, Lisa!

Sia pours her drink over Lisa's hair while Lisa is staring into Mose's eyes. Brittney and the others run to stop it but they are too late. They hold Sia back. Lisa stares at Mose, numb. He slowly approaches her.

MOSE: I'm sorry, I can explain.

Lisa slaps Mose.

MOSE: I tried to . . . I was gonna tell you.

LISA: Tell me what, that it was all a fuckin' dare?

MOSE: Look, you don't understand.

LISA: No, you don't understand! You don't know what it's like to have your father walk out on you, you don't know what it's like to move from school to school.

MOSE: You think this is easy for me? I don't know who I am anymore. I'm lost. Confused.

LISA: You have no idea.

MOSE: This is hard for me as well.

LISA: You're not the one that got used for a fuckin' dare!

MOSE: I don't care about the dare!

LISA: Bullshit! Everything you said was a lie. Fallen in love with me for who I am and not what I am? All the talks and the walks home? All a lie, Mose. Fuck you! I never wanna—

Mose kisses Lisa. We ain't talking no peck on the check, but those long kisses that feel like they last forever. Lisa struggles at first with the kiss and then eventually gives in. They stop and stare at each other for a while, then they realise everyone is around them. They slowly begin to look out and Mr. Jensen starts a slow clap with everyone eventually joining in.

MR. JENSEN: Ladies and gentlemen, your King and Queen!

Clap dies out and everyone disperses slowly offstage. Lighting changes. Lisa and Mose stand side by side facing the audience. Cast come back out for a big dance number.

The End

GAGA: THE UNMENTIONABLE

LOUISE TU`U

Gaga: The Unmentionable

Written by Louise Tu'u

About the author

Louise Tu'u is a producer and performer. With an interdisciplinary practice of over fifteen years in theatre, film, dance and the visual arts both in Niu Sila[1] and abroad, Tu'u's work has been described by critics as a 'contemporary Pacific performance extravaganza at it's best'. Leading We Should Practice[2] since 2009, Tu'u continues to live and make work in Aukilani, Niu Sila.

About the play

Gaga: The Unmentionable looks at the writer's mother tongue, Sāmoan, through the eyes and experiences of her first language teachers, her parents. Contrary to how it might appear, *Gaga: the Unmentionable* is not a tribute show or remotely related to Lady Gaga.

Gaga actually comes from the hacking of the Sāmoan word 'Gagana' which refers to the language. It's also pronounced 'nganga', not 'ga-ga'. Incidentally, Gagana is also a bird in Russian folklore with an iron beak and copper claws.

Acknowledgements

2011
Zahra Killeen-Chance and Christina Houghton, curators of the *Taste Me* show at Galatos where an excerpt of this work premiered.

---

1 New Zealand.
2 www.weshouldpractice.com.

2012
Paljon kiitoksia Minna Pesonen for the amazing translations of Louise's text and voice recording.
Jeff Henderson of Audio Foundation for the rehearsal venue and lights.
Sean Curham of Auckland Old Folks Association for the performance venue.
Campbell Farquhar for his wonderful videography.
My wonderful cast of Ilasa Galuvao and Nisha Madhan, who performed in both *Taste Me* and the debut season, Leki Jackson-Bourke, Aisea Latu and Eric Ripley and production guru Kate Burton who joined us for the Auckland Old Folks Association Hall season.

O taimi uma.
Mo ou matua, Lafitaga ma Sale Tu`u. Fa`afetai tele lava mo le alofa ma agalelei.
My brothers, Filisi and Charlie for having my back.
Brent Harris for your patience and love.
Maja Tu`u mo le alofa ma agamalie.

First performance
Gaga: The Unmentionable premiered at Auckland Old Folks Association Hall, Newton, Auckland City, New Zealand on Monday 3rd December, 2012.

Cast
USHERS: Aisea Latu and Eric Ripley
YOUNG WOMAN: Nisha Madhan
MIDDLE MAN: Leki Jackson-Bourke
SHORT WOMAN: Ilasa Galuvao
LOUISE TU`U: Louise Tu`u
ELDERLY WOMAN: Lafitaga Tu`u

Crew
WRITER/DIRECTOR: Louise Tu`u
PRODUCTION DESIGNER: Kate Burton

Gaga: The Unmentionable

Scene 1: The floor

An USHER distributes hot towels with a pair of tongs amongst the audience members while another usher collects them with a bucket. This bucket is then placed at the front of the playing area, always onstage, somewhere in the space.

Darkness onstage. White flour is sprinkled all over the floor. Lights come up and down incrementally at a very slow pace. A YOUNG WOMAN enters and smiles at the floor. She begins to play with the flour, lying on it and making snow angels with her body.

YOUNG WOMAN: In the beginning there was the darkness.

MIDDLE MAN enters and watches her silently. After a while, he kicks at the flour, startling her.

YOUNG WOMAN: The darkness was infinite, omniscient and powerful. Everyone feared the darkness.

Middle man continues to kick her, trying to egg her on. The young woman ignores him.

YOUNG WOMAN: Then the Gods came to talk to the darkness, who was very agitated.

Young woman sits up and puts out her hands in a slow and deliberate manner. She uses a different finger to represent each character in her story.

YOUNG WOMAN: 'Why are you agitated?' said the Gods. After a long silence, the darkness looked up and said, 'How did you know I was agitated?' The Gods said, 'We know everything.'

Middle man nods his head and tries to silently get the audience to agree with this.

YOUNG WOMAN: The darkness replied, 'Well what's this everything?' 'What do you mean?' said the Gods. 'We made you.' The darkness roared and sneezed. He snarled, 'Did you know that I have been nursing a cold for the past two days?' 'Well, when we said everything, we meant big things,' replied the confused but all-powerful Gods. 'This is a big thing,' snarled back the darkness. 'It may be a small thing to you but it means that every time I sneeze, people in their small huts in the developing world and condominiums and villas in the first world hear my might and suffer with my vivid absence of care, respect and personal hygiene for them, my mortals whom I care for and love.

Middle man is entranced by this nonsensical story and starts to form a letter A from the alphabet with his body. SHORT WOMAN joins him and they start performing the letters of the alphabet to the audience. The pair make it to B.

Young woman looks around in mild embarrassment, breaking out of her shamanistic state.

YOUNG WOMAN: I'm very sorry everyone . . .

Short woman and middle man are up to the letter C.

YOUNG WOMAN: . . . they seem to have forgotten that . . .

Short woman and middle man are up to the letter D.

YOUNG WOMAN: I think they are a few drafts behind and we actually cut that part of the show.

The pair are now up to E. Young woman decides to plead with them directly.

YOUNG WOMAN: If we could start again, it's alright.

Short woman and middle man are up to the letter F.

YOUNG WOMAN: It would really be a good idea. Guys, I really don't . . .

The pair keep going till about the letter G. Young woman goes to yell at them when classical music starts playing for about 20 seconds. This becomes the only thing that can be heard. The song is then abruptly cut off. Short woman brings a pair of Louise's father's work overalls to LOUISE TU`U, the writer and director who is sitting in the audience. She reluctantly puts them on. From where she is, she attempts to do handstands across to the other side of the stage.

LOUISE TU`U: No se mitä täällä tapahtuu on aika eriskummalista. Halusin luoda hyvää tarkoittavan työn, joka asettaa kielen sekä minun ja sinun suhteen kieleen kyseenalaiseksi, sekä pitää hauskaa. Tiedätkö, minä olen ilonpidon suuri fani. Me, sinä, ei voida keskittyä, jos ei ole mitään kiinnostavaa.¹

As she tries to do handstands and repeatedly fails, Louise Tu`u starts to peek at her hands and read her lines from there. The audience laugh and wonder whether what she is saying is a real language. Louise Tu`u points to the young woman. Lights are at 50 percent.

LOUISE TU`U: Näetko tāman naisen?²

The young woman looks up.

LOUISE TU`U: Esiintyjänä hän on todella loistava. Aina utelias, aina oikeudenmukainen. Hänen kanssaan on helppo tulla toimeen, laatu tavaraa.³

Young woman blushes and grins at Louise Tu`u, who smiles back. The others wait and look at her, expectantly.

---

1 So, what's happening here is quite usual. I wanted to create this well-meaning piece of work that questions language and my place in it, your place in it, and have some fun. I'm a big fan of fun, you see. It's hard to concentrate unless there's something interesting.
2 See this woman?
3 As a performer, she's great. Always inquisitive, always fair. Easy to get on with, top notch.

LOUISE TU'U: Tämä toinen nainen on myös upea, kosha hän reagoi todella hyvin toisiin esiintyjiin.[1]

The short woman beams and gives Louise the thumbs up.

LOUISE TU'U: Ja tama toinen tässa?[2]

The middle man looks up, hopeful.

LOUISE TU'U: Hänen innostuksessaan ei ole mitään vikaa.[3]

He runs over to hug Louise Tu'u and heads back to the group, high-fiving the other two. Louise looks over to ELDERLY WOMAN.

LOUISE TU'U: Varo hanta. Hän voi särkea sydämesi.

Middle man and short woman now appear and stand next to the young woman. The young woman goes offstage and brings back a roll of butcher's paper. Lights are at 70 percent. The roll is quite heavy. The short woman cuts up the paper, while the young woman watches. Taking a piece of paper, the short woman rolls it up tightly, spits on it, and throws it up onto the ceiling. Lights are at 96 percent. The middle man also spits on the paper and throws it up to the ceiling. Young woman exits.

LOUISE TU'U: Nyt tällä hetkellä tapahtuu se, että tiimi tekee yhteistyötä. Se on tosi hienoa ja hyvin uusi seelantilaista. He yrittävät hetken ajan saada tämän työn kasaan, mutta se on hieman mutkikasta tästä lähtien. No ei se mitään, toivottavasti voit hyvin ja nautit (esityksestä).[4]

The cast look at Louise. The short woman continues to make the letter H, along with the middle man. They continue on until the letter L, at which point she stops and walks off. Lights are 80 percent.

---

[1] This other woman is also great as she responds really well to the other performers.
[2] And this one here?
[3] You just can't fault his enthusiasm.
[4] Now what's happening is that the team are collaborating. It's cool and very New Zealand. They'll try for a while with this work to get it up and running but it's pretty convoluted from here on in. Anyhoo, hope you're well and enjoy.

Scene 2: Village life

'Someday My Prince Will Come' by Chet Baker plays. The young woman and the short woman, who is now dressed in the overalls, waltz back and forth across the stage.

The middle man is skipping with a skipping rope and dressed only in an ie lavalava. Wherever she is sitting, elderly woman performs a slow siva, oblivious to everyone else on stage.

MIDDLE MAN: It's completely normal for us to wear this – summer, spring, winter, autumn. Though in the Islands, that's all the same.

SHORT WOMAN: I used to get up every morning and chase the chickens away. It was a hard life, hard times, not like now. I get a rectangle, put the circle and a beam comes up. Pretty things make me look old.

YOUNG WOMAN: I would grab a pawpaw and point a stick at it, then voila! There was breakfast.

SHORT WOMAN: Only lazy people would do that from your village.

MIDDLE MAN: At least I have a village. They left you on the windscreen of someone's car, like bird shit.

SHORT WOMAN: I heard that's why you can't speak English properly – because someone punched you in the mouth too much.

MIDDLE MAN: I can have you and your family kicked out like that.

SHORT WOMAN: Go on, do it then. You've never wanted me to be here except because.

MIDDLE MAN: Except because? That's why you work in a factory.

SHORT WOMAN: Eehhhh! You better watch your mouth before I come over and touch it.

MIDDLE MAN: Shut your mouth before I ring up immigration to come and deport you back.

Young woman comes over and performs the letter I to try and stop the growing antagonism.

YOUNG WOMAN: C'mon guys. Take it easy. There's people everywhere.

SHORT WOMAN: You're lucky my friend's here. Otherwise I would have ...

MIDDLE MAN: What? Come on, do it! You took my chips that I left onstage and ate all of them. You ... you bitch!

SHORT WOMAN: What are you looking at, you big boogey eyes? Go on, what's wrong? Haven't you seen an All Blacks' sister before? C'mon say it, say my surname!

MIDDLE MAN: Yes, everybody, you're looking at Conrad Smith's fiancée.

SHORT WOMAN: Shut up, you fob. That's between me and Connie.

YOUNG WOMAN: You didn't tell me that.

Young woman brings out her ie and waves it between middle man and short woman, who have now transformed into raging bulls.

YOUNG WOMAN: Fight! Fight! Fight! Fight!

Middle man and short woman now turn their attentions toward young woman and come towards her.

LOUISE TU'U (split focus): Ainoa kakkonen blah blah kolme neljä viisi kuusi seitsemän kahdeksan ainoa ainoa ainoa blah kahdeksan kahdeksan viisi blah blah bah yhdeksikkö kaksikymmentä yksitoista sata sata tuhat ainoa kakkonen blah kakkonen neljäkymmentä blah viisi seitsemäntoista.[1]

---

[1] Only number two blah blah three four five six seven eight only only only blah eight eight five blah blah bah number nine twenty eleven a hundred a hundred a thousand only number two blah number two forty blah five seventeen.

Scene 3: The letter

Middle man is now wearing the overalls and is spotlit. He has his laptop on his lap. The three woman are watching him. Middle man pretends not to see them and reads out aloud as he types.

MIDDLE MAN (reading out the letter from the laptop): Dear Oprah, How are you? I write to you because I watch your show every day and am a big fan. Every day you have a big gift for people under their seats. I live in New Zealand for 45 years now, I watch your show every day for 25 years. It is very good. I retire now and live at home with my wife. I ask my daughter to write this letter to you but she say I have to write it because I go to school now. I ask you now for a car, not too expensive but a car now that I am old. I already have two cars but I would really like a new car because the other cars are old. I watch Dr Phil now and see you have OWN network. You work hard and you're young so that's very good. Even though you have no husband and no children. It's alright Oprah, I'm not nosey. I would like a big car like a Lexus or a pick-up. A nice car for an old man like me.

Thank you very much, Oprah. God bless you and write to me soon.

Thank you.
Old Man,
Grey Lynn,
Auckland,
New Zealand.

Scene 4: Contemporary dance middle

A soundtrack of chirping birds can be heard. Young woman, short woman and elderly woman are all seated facing each other in a triangle, opening out to the audience. The elderly woman nervously rubs her hands together while the young woman looks at the other two with a bemused smile. The short woman looks straight ahead, oblivious. The elderly woman becomes more and more agitated, trying not to look at the audience. The short woman is concentrating on the opposite wall. A miti (short kissing noise) can be heard from the other side of the room. Both the elderly woman and young woman move their heads to the noise. The short woman stands up, with the other two following suit.

SHORT WOMAN: One, two, three, four.

The trio extend their respective right arms up, down, right then use their left arms up, down, left and continue this dance, watching each other.

SHORT WOMAN: I smiled at four people today and they smiled back. I am loved.

ELDERLY WOMAN: I don't want to say anything yet. Not while they're here.

Dancing continues.

YOUNG WOMAN: I will now do a traditional dance from my country.

SHORT WOMAN: I smiled at four people today and they smiled back. I am loved.

ELDERLY WOMAN: Two tables sat next to each other and laughed.

Dancing continues.

SHORT WOMAN: Ilasa prepares herself to sing.

The elderly woman starts to move of her own accord. The young woman imitates her.

YOUNG WOMAN: Please help us look after the floor. Do not drag yourselves across it. We are performing, not you.

Dancing continues. 'DJ Got Us Falling in Love' by Usher plays. The elderly woman cannot help herself and gets down in the worst possible way. The short woman follows them.

'Wanna be Starting Something' by Michael Jackson plays. The elderly woman struts her stuff. The short woman moves beside her with the young woman on the other side. they start to dance in unison, using their peripheral vision to keep in time together.

'Charmer' by Kings of Leon plays. The elderly woman chills out and pulls faces, with the others imitating her.

Scene 5: Variables

The middle man brings on a whiteboard, chair and marker pens. The elderly woman, exhausted from dancing, sits on the chair and reapplies her lipstick. Louise Tu`u enters. She pats the elderly woman who squirms. Louise Tu`u takes a breath. Elderly woman frowns at her. They both dance a siva side by side.

ELDERLY WOMAN: Ua, a? Ua uma lau show valea?[1]

Elderly woman then remembers the audience and lovingly touches Louise Tu`u, smiling broadly.

ELDERLY WOMAN: E tigā lava ona ou fa`asamoa atu, palagi, ae e te le nanu mai. Va`ai ou te tū i luga ma sasa oe i luma o tagata.[2]

LOUISE TU`U: I can't.

ELDERLY WOMAN: Se a se a e te fesili ia a`u e fai le isi show pepelo, ua iloa? Ua tiga o`u vae.[3]

LOUISE TU`U: Just let me explain this then I'll get off promise.

ELDERLY WOMAN: Ua tele taimi ou te talitonu ai ia oe ae e te pepelo mai lava ia te a`u. O a`u o lou tina, ou te lē valea. A fai e te toe sau i lo tatou aiga, sau mai aumai sou oso. Ae aua le li mai na`o ou nifo. E na`o mea valea ou te fai taimi uma mo oe. O fea a`u grandchildren, eh?[4]

Louise Tu`u exits offstage and brings back the short woman. The elderly woman immediately smiles and gestures to her to come over. She kisses the short woman on the cheek.

---

1 Well, is your dumb show finished?
2 Even though I speak to you in Sāmoan palagi and you don't reply to me in Sāmoan, watch out that I don't stand up and smack you in front of the audience.
3 Don't ever ask me to be in your dumb show again, OK? My leg hurts.
4 So many times I've believed you but you keep lying to me. I am your mother not some idiot. The next time you come over, please bring something, not just your teeth to smile with. You only do stupid things all the time. Where are my grandchildren, eh?

ELDERLY WOMAN: Oi hello Ilasa! O a mai?[1]

SHORT WOMAN: Malo tinā! Louise you'd better hurry up.

LOUISE TU'U: I'm trying mate. She tried to give me a hiding.

SHORT WOMAN: Out here? Don't lie. She wouldn't be that stupid. There's palagis here.

LOUISE TU'U: I didn't even have time to tell her.

ELDERLY WOMAN: Ua a. Ua uma?[2]

Louise Tu'u looks pleadingly at the short woman.

SHORT WOMAN: Fa'amalie atu ua fai sina leva . . .[3]

She looks offstage and whispers loudly.

SHORT WOMAN: Come and distract her.

The young woman, who now wears the overalls, and middle man form a straight line, facing the audience.

YOUNG WOMAN: Mmmmmmmm.

MIDDLE MAN: Give it up for Nnnnnelly!

YOUNG WOMAN: I'm talking about . . . oh, oh, oh oh, oh oh oh.

Louise Tu'u and the short woman look on.

LOUISE TU'U: When did it get this desperate?

---

[1] Oh hello, Llasa, how are you?
[2] Well, are we finished?
[3] Sorry that it's been so long . . .

SHORT WOMAN: When you got your mum involved. It's crazy.

LOUISE TU'U: Nah, it isn't. It was fun.

SHORT WOMAN: Yeah it's so cool for her she wants to beat you up onstage.

MIDDLE MAN: Wassup peeeeeople rhymes with . . .

YOUNG WOMAN: Question my Q my Queen mean as.

YOUNG WOMAN: Raaaaaaaa . . . RRRRRaring to go.

LOUISE TU'U: She said she was gonna beat me at home. Out here, it's already way too performative.

SHORT WOMAN: I've got an idea. Just let them finish.

YOUNG MAN: Sassy Sassy Silly with an S.

MIDDLE MAN: T is the tip of my tippy tip toes.

> *Elderly woman igis (pinches) Louise Tu'u and smiles at the audience. The others jump in with beat-boxing noises and wave their arms together in a synchronised fashion. The elderly woman smiles. Louise Tu'u walks over to a whiteboard, which is offstage, and grabs a pen from the middle man. She starts drawing up a bar graph.*

SHORT WOMAN: What Louise is showing you is the progress of the show. Right about now, she's assessing that exactly half of you are not interested, a quarter of you are thinking about what wine you will be ordering from the various bars nearby and the remaining quarter are here because you got comps.

Pause.

SHORT WOMAN: I know what you're thinking. We can't afford to be so negative in such times.

Louise Tu`u turns around and tries to see into the audience. She then goes back to the whiteboard, scribbling more.

SHORT WOMAN: She reckons some of you will leave soon but secretly want to know if something melodramatic happens.

Louise Tu`u pauses and stares at the audience.

SHORT WOMAN: She reckons you'll leave now.

Elderly woman's phone recording plays for exactly 35 seconds.

Scene 6: Communal dance

*Young woman and middle man interact. Short woman encounters them.
A man whistles outside.*

Scene 7: Twenty uses

YOUNG WOMAN: You may be wondering what I would do without this.

Young woman points to her ie lavalava.

YOUNG WOMAN: I wonder that myself.

SHORT WOMAN: You know that I was wondering that from the other side.

YOUNG WOMAN: Were you really?

SHORT WOMAN: Yes, a marvellous piece of . . .

Pause.

SHORT WOMAN: What is it exactly?

YOUNG WOMAN: Funny you should ask.

Young woman puts it over her head.

SHORT WOMAN: Why, where have you gone, my friend?

YOUNG WOMAN: I'm right here. You just can't see me.

SHORT WOMAN: Amazing! What else can you do?

YOUNG WOMAN: Well, with Auckland's unpredictable weather, you get a two-for one.

SHORT WOMAN: How do you mean?

YOUNG WOMAN: When you walk outside, usually it will be sunny so you can use this as a fan.

SHORT WOMAN: Marvellous!

YOUNG WOMAN: Then when it inevitably turns to custard, it becomes an umbrella.

As the two women hold up all four corners to shield themselves, they make accompanying rain noises that intensify as they get it up.

SHORT WOMAN: I love how it's waterproof.

YOUNG WOMAN: I did that this morning. Lucky I brought my washing in. That Gore-Tex stuff works a treat.

SHORT WOMAN: The first thing I thought when I looked at it was how culturally appropriate it could be.

YOUNG WOMAN: How do you mean?

SHORT WOMAN: Well, let's say one day I need to go to another fa`alavelave. I can use it as a nifo oti for my dance to gather money.

She starts to dance and tosses the lavalava into the air, incorporating it into her taupou dance.

YOUNG WOMAN: They call it crowdfunding now.

SHORT WOMAN: Oh yes, and when I go to a wedding, I can wear it as a sari.

As the short woman finishes her dance, the young woman sneaks underneath her and entangles herself in the sari

YOUNG WOMAN: Or I can cross boundaries and wear it as a turban.

SHORT WOMAN: How did the move go?

YOUNG WOMAN: We did it this weekend. Living in town, living the dream.

They both sit down and lie down, facing the audience.

YOUNG WOMAN: But the thing that I miss is being outside. Despite the regular rubbish weather, despite the handy foodcourt and hedonistic parties, sometimes I just want to be outside.

'Feels like rain' by Aaj Mera Jee Kardaa starts to play.

YOUNG WOMAN: When I close my eyes sometimes, I feel like I'm outside on a scorching day, filled with humidity. That I'm transported on my magic carpet to a faraway land.

Young woman grabs the ie and spreads it on the ground ceremoniously.

YOUNG WOMAN: Close your eyes with me.

The short woman closes her eyes and they hold hands together.

YOUNG WOMAN: Can you picture it? Can you smell it?

SHORT WOMAN: Yes, yes, I can! It's unbelievable. Utterly adorable.

YOUNG WOMAN: Of course, you can.

Pause.

YOUNG WOMAN: Welcome to my interior garden.

Scene 8: Il lavoro

Middle man is reading a book onstage and sits on the ie lavalava. He sips from a glass of water and picks up a microphone.

MIDDLE MAN: You know how the octopus got those marks on its head? Now this is what the old people from the old times say in Sāmoa when my wife and I were growing up.

He uses the whiteboard and wipes the previous writings off.

MIDDLE MAN: One day the rat wanted to get across a pool of water. It was too big so it saw the octopus who he knew from somewhere else.

So, the rat said to the octopus, 'You are such a good person.' The octopus said, 'Yes, I am.'

And the rat said, 'Well I need to visit my cousins on the other side.'

'Well lucky for you,' said the octopus. 'It's my day off.'

So the octopus lets the rat sit on his head and dropped him off to the other side, where he want to go. After the rat got off his head, he said to the octopus, 'What's that stuff on your head?'

Middle man waits for a reaction.

ELDERLY WOMAN: He said, 'That's shit on your head.'

MIDDLE MAN: This is not your story.

ELDERLY WOMAN: O le tala o le fe`e ma le isumu. O le a lou feau i lenei tala?[1]

Elderly woman looks at the audience.

---

[1] This is the story of the octopus and the rat. Where are you in this story?

Scene 9: Crank shaft (Alternative ending I)

ELDERLY WOMAN (to audience): Lucky for you, you are all you can't see any Sāmoan in this show because you pay for it.

Some audience members murmur that they didn't pay for their ticket but smile as the elderly woman's gaze falls on them. She walks onstage. Louise Tu`u grabs a chair for her.

LOUISE TU`U: There you go Mum.

Elderly woman smiles at her. An extension cord is dropped off onto the floor gently by the middle man, landing by her chair. She frowns but quickly remembers the audience and smiles again, as she looks up at middle man.

ELDERLY WOMAN: Thank you son. I want to tell you my story because it's real. When Louise was small I was fit. I had four jobs. One's a full-time job with 40 hours a week and three part-time job. I was working in the factory called Venluree to make a venetian blind, vertical blind, Holland blind.

I was making them for 30 years. And my first part-time job I was cleaning in Auckland University, me and my friend next door. We had two days; two morning a week start from 2 o'clock and finish 5 o'clock in the morning. And my next two part-time job I was working in Mt Albert for the Baptist Church. I was working there for two nights, 11 o'clock at night till 7 o'clock in the morning.

And my last part-time job, they all the same time for the full-time job, I was working in Karangahape Road by that time for that a restaurant was famous. Working there for weekend, Saturdays and Sundays, 5 o'clock to 8 o'clock. And the rest of some hours I stay home to look after the family, especially the young one, that's the baby of the family Louise.

Elderly woman looks at the extension cord and decides to use it.

ELDERLY WOMAN: This is the extension cord; I think everybody knows the extension cord me.

I only say some few explanation. I used the extension cord if I used to vacuum, not enough cord, so I use this one. So as washing machine, not enough cord, using this. I let you; everybody to know how to use the extension cord.

The cast members sing the taualuga which excites the elderly woman who dances a siva Sāmoa.

Scene 9: Crank shaft (Alternative ending II)

The elderly woman remains onstage. The bucket remains in front. Louise Tu'u drops off an extension cord. The elderly woman scowls.

ELDERLY WOMAN: Ave ese lenei mea. E matagā.[1]

LOUISE TU'U: No you have to do it, Mum. It's the last bit, promise.

Elderly woman performs a taualuga with the cord, talking to it, leaving it on the ground untouched.

O Le Fa'aiuga (The End)

---

1 Take that thing off. It's embarrassing.

Credits and acknowledgements

Publishers • Evotia Tamua, Tony Murrow
Auckland Council • Arts and Culture
Auckland Libraries • Elenoa Mo`a Sili-Mati
Playmarket • Murray Lynch
Photography • Evotia Tamua
Project Management • Rebecca Kunin, Evotia Tamua
Sales and Marketing • Evotia Tamua
Social Media • Shanlea Hibbs
Book Production • Amy Tansell
Book Design • Amy Tansell
Cover Design • Tony Murrow
Editing • Louise Russell
Proofing • Fredrick Loloa Ālatini (Tongan),
    Avikaila Sopoitulagi Tilialo (Sāmoan),
    Tutagaloa Tose Tuhipa (Niuean)
Printing • Lightning Source

LITTLE ISLAND PRESS

little island press is a community publisher
and social enterprise based in New Zealand

little island aims to connect people and communities through books

www.facebook.com/littleislandpress/

littleisland.co.nz

www.ingramcontent.com/pod-product-compliance
Lightning Source LLC
Chambersburg PA
CBHW020109020526
44112CB00033B/1106